Lessons
from
Armed
America

High Praise for Kathy Jackson and Mark Walters!

"I have worked with Kathy Jackson and Mark Walters for over five years. Not only are they extremely knowledgeable when it comes to self defense and personal protection, but they are two of the staunchest defenders of freedom and liberty that I know. Mark and Kathy write from the heart because they truly care about people... and that is why I have complete trust in their advice and recommendations."

– Tim Schmidt
Publisher - Concealed Carry Magazine
Founder - United States Concealed Carry Association –

"Self preservation is the first law of nature. It is common sense that firearms even the odds for weaker humans who otherwise would be defenseless against human predators. As the old saying goes, "God created men (and women). Sam Colt made them equal". Kathy Jackson's and Mark Walter's *Lessons from Armed America* is an essential primer on self preservation. Buy this book, read it thoroughly, and become prepared to deal with reality, as unwelcome as it may be."

– Bruce N. Eimer, Ph.D.
Board Certified, Licensed Clinical Psychologist
Founder, www.DefensiveHandguns.com
www.PersonalDefenseSolutions.net–

"How much better to learn from the experiences of others than making one's own painful mistakes! In Lessons from Armed America, we have a tremendous educational resource. First comes an account of how a violent crime occurred; it is followed by analysis of how it could have been prevented, stopped short, or survived. This is a powerful format, enjoyable to read, and packed full of valuable lessons."

– Gila Hayes
Operations Manager, The Firearms Academy of Seattle
Author of "Effective Defense" and "Personal Defense for Women" –

"This book blew me away with useful info on self defense! Kathy and Mark centered the bullseye! It's not just a good read, it's absolute, need-to-know info on how to protect yourself and your family. Read it and enjoy!"

– Skip Coryell
Founder, Second Amendment March
Author of "Blood in the Streets" –

Published by White Feather Press, LLC in 2009

ISBN   978-0-9822487-6-8

Printed in the United States of America

Cover design by Ron Bell of AdVision Design Group (www.advisiondesigngroup.com)

Disclaimer

The authors of this book assume that you, the reader, are an adult human being capable of making your own choices and taking responsibility for same. If you are not an adult, or are not capable of taking responsibility for your own choices, STOP. Do not read anything else in this book. The authors have made a reasonable, good-faith effort to assure that the book is accurate and contains good advice, but we hereby advise the reader that the authors are normal human beings who make the normal number of human mistakes. If something in this book sounds stupid or dangerous to you, don't do it. The authors accept absolutely no responsibility whatsoever for anything you might say or do as a result of reading any material in this book. Live your own life!

White Feather Press

Reaffirming Faith in God, Family, and Country!

Contents

Lessons from Armed America

True stories of men and women who defended themselves and their families

Kathy Jackson

&

Mark Walters

Dedication

It is with profound gratitude that I dedicate this book to my family, without whom nothing else would matter. I thank God every day for bringing each of you into my life – and pray every day that He will keep you safe in His loving arms.

–Kathy Jackson–

This book would not have been possible without the assistance of some amazing people.

To Tim Schmidt: Thank you for the opportunity you gave me to write.

To my co-author and managing editor Kathy Jackson for coming along at the right time in my life.

To those of you whose encouragement meant so much to me, you know who you are.

To my parents simply for being my parents.

To my children. Thank you for giving me the courage and strength to be your dad. Without you, nothing else matters.

Finally, to the survivors. Without your dedication, honesty and strength, none of this would have been possible. May your bravery and courage be an inspiration to every reader to take control of their own lives. To you, I dedicate these pages.

–Mark Walters –

Foreword

by Massad Ayoob

It's always an honor to be asked to write a foreword for a book in your field, and it's particularly so in this case.

I've known Kathy Jackson for years, first as a student and later as a co-instructor. I've been a guest on Mark's radio show and Podcast. They both do good, and important, work.

Kathy was a brilliant student who became a brilliant instructor in her own right. Reviewing the manuscript here showed me just how deeply Kathy had internalized what she learned from me, and of course from others. If you don't read, you can't write; if you don't learn, you can't teach. Kathy Jackson was and is an insightful and incisive learner, and that has done much to make her the patient, knowledgeable, informative writer and trainer that she is today. For years now, her website www.corneredcat. com has been high on my list of recommended study for my own readers and students, and while I recommend it to people of both genders, I've found it particularly useful for women. I've watched her learn…I've watched her teach… I've seen her shoot (100% qualification scores on demand!) and I've read how she has made a compendium of her knowledge here and elsewhere. This woman is serious, and she has it nailed.

I've both read and listened to Mark, and it struck me in reviewing the manuscript of this book that even though I'd heard many of the personal experiences "from the horse's mouth" on

Mark's Podcast, seeing the detail he was able to bring out in his written version put more critical detail into the minds of all of us learners who have read, and will read, the book you're holding in your hands. We've all heard the old saying, "The Devil is in the details." We would do well to bear in mind that the great architect Ludwig Mies van der Rohe also said, "God is in the details." Mark Walters is also serious, and he also has it nailed.

It's the details that save you. Understanding the details of how violent encounters unfold, and the details of the history of the survival of the strong versus the death and crippling of the helpless. Understanding the details of the law, in a way that can allow you to act without hesitation instead of pausing to ask yourself "Am I allowed to, uh, hurt this guy?" in a moment when "he or she who hesitates" truly will be "lost."

Mark and Kathy have taken a new approach to ground some others of us have covered before. I've been writing about the legal, ethical, and psychological aspects of the use of defensive deadly force for decades, including my 1980 book In the Gravest Extreme. Others have since written books on that topic. I was the first to do a series of gunfight analyses in a periodical, American Handgunner magazine's long-running series called "Ayoob Files." And the first to do a book collecting such, titled with my usual lack of imagination, Ayoob Files: the Book. That's been done by others, too, notably the excellent work of Chris Bird and of Robert Waters, and the insightful studies of David Klinger and of Dr. Alexis Artwohl and Loren Christiansen. All are available through Police Bookshelf, PO Box 122, Concord, NH 03302.

But Kathy and Mark did something that makes me want to slap my palm against my forehead and exclaim, "Why didn't I think of that?!?" What they did was to combine the two.

Kathy does the "Here's what you need to know" part. Mark does the "Here's how it actually went down in this case" part. Together they become a book-length series of object lessons. The theory is starkly, instructively juxtaposed with the reality.

Whether you're new to the concept of armed defense or have long since made it a part of a prudent lifestyle, you'll find much that is useful in this book. Read it the way Kathy and Mark wrote it: that is, don't just look at it, but study it for its lessons.

They are lessons that can save lives, and this book speaks for itself on that.

Good luck, and stay safe.

Massad Ayoob
Live Oak, Florida
August, 2009

Chapter 1 - All Bets were Off!

Mark Walters

As a season ticket holder and Tampa Bay Buccaneer fan, I had spent my Sunday afternoon on November 17, 2002 cheering on my home team in the company of 65,527 other screaming NFL fans. For the first time in many years, we had quite a bit to cheer about in Tampa those days; we had a winning football team, a team that would go on to win the Super Bowl that season. Monday mornings would arrive too quickly for the local NFL fans. The alarm clock always had a unique way of ringing slightly louder the day after a Sunday home game.

Lately, though, I hadn't needed to use that trusty alarm clock. I had a new one that seemed to wake me up without having to set it and this one worked on a schedule all her own. Her name is Lindsey and on this particular Monday morning she would be just 16 days old. No matter the circumstances, she always seemed to know when daddy needed to get up and prepare for the long work day ahead.

She didn't come with a user's manual and for the first time in my adult life I felt totally helpless and truly overwhelmed. She would spend her first hours of life and the next four days in the neonatal intensive care unit with breathing difficulties and it was a blessing when she was cleared to come home. As unsure of myself as I was and as scared as I was with my newfound responsibilities, there was one thing that I did know the moment I saw her open her eyes and look up at me. It was instinctive and it was unmistakable. I knew that I would ferociously defend her with my life and with any means possible, from anything or anyone that might intend to do her harm.

I had taken my own self-defense what I thought to be very seriously by simply owning a gun since an unnerving incident several years earlier when a man passed me on a city street apparently upset that I was only travelling 10 mph over the posted speed limit. As his vehicle illegally passed and then slowed beside me, I noticed the flash of a large silver handgun. I cringed and waited for the glass to shatter. He stopped in front of me and opened his driver door slightly without exiting his vehicle, and I pulled backwards and reversed direction so I could continue on my way unharmed. Two months later I had a Florida concealed carry license and a second new gun.

I had begun practicing regularly with my handguns since that event, but never took the ultimate step to carry my gun with me everywhere I went, whenever I went, regardless of the circumstances. I found myself carrying when it was convenient or comfortable and if a criminal wanted my wallet and my life he had a 50/50 chance of running into an armed victim. Apparently I needed a refresher course and it would only be the luck of the draw that I chambered a round in my .45-caliber Glock model 36, holstered it and tucked it securely inside my waistband the morning of November 18, 2002.

I remember noticing how the weather had recently changed from the overwhelming humidity of late fall to the cooler and drier days of early winter as I stepped outside my home that morning. Starting my car and glancing downward at the dashboard clock, I noticed that it was somewhat earlier than usual as I pulled out of the driveway just slightly after 6 am, while it was still dark. I began my 20-minute ride to work, a drive that would take me through one of the worst neighborhoods in town.

Approximately 25 square miles in size and bordering the University of South Florida (USF) to the east and Interstate 275 to the west, "Suitcase City," as the locals refer to it, has the highest crime rate in the city of Tampa. The area derives its notorious nickname from the transient nature of its residents, due in large part to a glut of cheap apartment complexes surrounding USF and originally intended as off-campus student housing. As University enrollment grew over the years, it became a commuter school, leaving dozens of neighboring apartment homes vacant and available to lower income residents.

Like many of America's lower-income urban enclaves, Suitcase City suffers from a drug problem that by its very nature leads to various types of crime ranging from petty thefts and burglaries to robberies and murder. Because my office bordered the area, and because I spent so much of my time either driving through or working near this section of town, I rarely gave it much thought other than to stay alert and on my toes as I passed through.

Departing the upscale suburbs, I headed to work. Heading west on Fletcher Avenue through the heart of Suitcase City towards the intersection of Nebraska Avenue that morning, I noticed a dark colored SUV that appeared to be stopped near the intersection in the right lane ahead of me. I glanced over my left shoulder and maneuvered my vehicle into the left lane and out of the path of the apparently stalled SUV. I had two options

3

when driving this way to work: I could head straight through the light or make a left turn onto Nebraska Avenue. Either direction would take me to my final destination, so my decision would be based on the timing of the approaching traffic signal. If the light remained green I would go straight, but if it turned yellow I would move into the left lane and catch the arrow, saving myself a few seconds.

Keeping my eyes on the stopped SUV, I decided to go straight as cars began piling up in the left turn lane like a log jam. Then I heard it. SCREEEEEEEEECH! The air became heavy with the thickness of blue tire smoke as I approached the intersection. I grabbed the steering wheel hard and instinctively slammed on my brakes to avoid a collision as the seemingly parked SUV had roared to life, turning violently to the left and coming to a dead stop in front of and perpendicular to my vehicle.

As the rubber smoke drifted slowly past my vehicle and engulfed the cars stopped to my left, I could now identify the SUV as a Jeep Cherokee with dark tinted windows, a common sight in Florida. The Cherokee was sitting directly in front of me, unable to move forward as it was blocked by a line of traffic that had backed up in the turn lane.

I instinctively motioned to the driver hidden behind the safety of his darkened windows in what I'm sure some folks would refer to as a "not so nice gesture." Although I'm not exactly sure what words I used to describe his erratic driving behavior, I can assure you that they've never been uttered in a Disney cartoon. With traffic backing up behind me and on all sides, I was now trapped.

As I sat and pondered how fortunate the driver of the Jeep was that I didn't slam him into his next life, I observed the front

4

door of the Cherokee begin to open. As it touched the front bumper of my vehicle, I noticed a tall black male slide out of the 2-foot crack of the open driver's door while another black male walked towards the front of the opposite side of the Jeep, apparently exiting the vehicle from the passenger side. The driver, standing in front of my vehicle and slightly off of my front left bumper, gestured towards me and yelled what I remember to be "You next, motherf---er" while wrapping his right hand in what appeared to be a shirt of some sort. What had started just seconds earlier as a benign traffic tie-up seemingly caused by a reckless driver was now unfolding into a very dangerous situation.

Feeling the unmistakable rush of adrenaline as my heart began to pound, I would later come to realize that I was experiencing the body's instinctive reaction of "fight or flight." Having nowhere to run with my automobile boxed in like a caged animal, I unlatched my seatbelt with my right hand and quickly lifted my untucked shirt above and behind the grip of my .45 caliber Glock 36.

With the driver of the Jeep now turning his attention away from me, I watched in amazement as he began fiercely beating the passenger window of a Toyota which was blocking his way, while his partner violently jumped and pounded on the hood of the same car. I could see the driver, a woman, screaming frantically with nowhere to go. What seemed like an eternity as this surreal event was unfolding in front of me was actually only seconds old, if that.

As I fixated on what I was witnessing, the driver turned his attention and unbridled rage toward me. Failing to break the passenger window with his cloth-covered hand, the driver turned rapidly and violently toward my windshield. Motioning with one hand in my direction, only feet from my windshield and re-wrapping his other hand in the shirt, he yelled something to the effect of "I told you, you were next, bitch." All bets were off. I was going home today at his expense, if necessary.

I had yet to see a weapon from either the driver or his accomplice; however, they had the advantage of size and position, and there were two of them to one of me. I was not going to wait until it was too late. As the driver moved one step forward towards my vehicle, I unholstered my weapon with my right hand and in one swift motion placed my outstretched arms upon the steering wheel. With a solid two-handed grip and the muzzle of my handgun touching the cold morning glass of the windshield, I leveled the .45 caliber Glock directly at the driver's chest.

A raging river of adrenaline pumped through my veins as the two of us made eye contact for the first time. Here I was in the middle of Fletcher Avenue in Tampa, Florida, in the early morning dawn, pointing my fully loaded and chambered handgun directly at another human being, ready to fire. As long as I live I will never forget the look on that punk's face. He was caught. I had the drop on him. He blinked.

"Move the car, bitch, move the car," yelled the passenger, pointing at the petrified woman behind the wheel of the car blocking his path, completely unaware of the loaded handgun aimed at his partner's chest. I moved my eyes from the man in front of me now standing fully erect and staring in my direction and towards his accomplice. Pointing my weapon at his face from approximately fifteen feet away, I quickly returned to cover the driver directly off of my left bumper who now stood motionless as if his feet were stuck in dried cement.

I can only imagine what the open muzzle of that compact Glock must have looked like to these men. My mind raced fervently and only bits and pieces of memory remain from the massive adrenaline dump I was experiencing.

I had recently completed a course in multiple attackers training a few weeks earlier and now found myself facing two individuals. "Watch his hands," I thought, "Watch his hands. His eyes won't harm you but his hands will. Watch his HANDS." Completely oblivious to my surroundings except for the two men in front of me, I had made the decision to kill them both, if necessary. Thoughts were racing through my mind: "What if I fire and miss?" "Will I permanently lose my hearing from inside the closed car?"

In one sweeping motion, the driver turned away from me and glanced over his right shoulder towards his passenger, who was now staring at me like a deer caught in a spotlight. At the same moment, he swung his shirt-clad right fist and arm into the air above him as if riding a bucking bronco. Looking back at me and yelling an inaudible comment to his passenger, he stepped slowly backwards, reaching with his left hand for the open car door a few steps to his left and behind him, his right arm still in the air as if to surrender and admit defeat.

Moving my handgun to follow the driver, I realized I had lost sight of the passenger as he re-entered the vehicle from the other side. Keeping my eyes trained on the driver and unable to hear his commands to his passenger, I continued to follow him with my muzzle until he stepped backwards into the Cherokee and behind the wheel of the SUV.

As the driver slammed his door and the tinted windows remained up, I lost sight of the two men inside the SUV. The

Cherokee lurched forward and nudged the Toyota gently out of the way, opening a gap wide enough for it to fit through. As quickly as it had begun it would end in a plume of bluish-white tire smoke as the Jeep Cherokee sped off in the opposite direction.

Shaking, I put my handgun on my lap, then glanced up to see the left-turn signal fade from red to green. Looking over to my left, I watched the Toyota speed away through the intersection as if nothing had occurred, the driver and her automobile disappearing into the morning light like ghosts in the foggy cemetery of a Stephen King novel.

A loud beep and a quick roar behind me reminded me that my light had now turned green and ironically it was me that was now holding up traffic. I continued on the five-minute drive to my office, walked inside and sat quietly in my chair. Within moments I was shaking terribly, sweating profusely and fighting a nauseating headache.

The incessant telephone ringing in the background reminded me that my workday had begun and I tried desperately to focus on my purpose for being there. It didn't work. By 1:30 PM I had left the office and driven two blocks south, where I purchased a snubnosed .357 revolver from an overpriced but conveniently located gun shop. For some reason the purchase of another new gun made me feel better.

Prior to leaving work that day I had placed a call to a Hillsborough County sheriff's deputy who had for years worked in the same office building as I. Describing the situation to the best of my memory, I was assured that I had done nothing wrong under Florida law and had indeed acted in self-defense within

Florida statutes. Her comments were reassuring, but had little impact on my forever-changed psyche.

Since that morning in November of 2002, I rarely leave my home unarmed. It does not matter where I go, what I do or whom I am with. You would never know it and I will never tell you but if you are in my presence, you are likely only inches away from my loaded handgun. And because I had made the decision not to be a victim prior to that balmy November morning, my daughter still has her daddy.

As the years have ticked by since the incident against me occurred, I have conjured up many theories about what had actually happened on that early November morning. Did the SUV driver intentionally target the Toyota that was attacked that morning? Is that why the Cherokee driver sat in the right lane at a dead stop? In retrospect it seems almost as if the driver knew the woman in the Toyota would happen upon that exact spot at that exact time. I wondered for months if it was some type of domestic dispute or stalking incident.

More important, during conversations about the incident, friends and relatives alike have asked me if I would have pulled the trigger that morning. My answer is a simple one: yes. Yes, I would have pulled the trigger and yes, I would have shot them both and continued firing until they were down. I would have continued firing until the threat they posed against me was over – and yes, I would have reloaded if necessary to continue firing until the threat was truly gone.

If my actions to stop the attack against me resulted in death, so be it. I was then, and I continue to be now, ready to take the life of another human being attempting to harm my loved ones or me. I have been tested. The thought that I am capable of such action does not bother me in the least and as a result of that frightening incident I am at peace with my decision to carry a gun. I am at peace with my capability to take another life to defend my own.

I hope and pray every day that I never find myself in another situation as dangerous as I found myself that morning. I am comforted that years of reflection have taught me that I did nothing wrong. Driving to work to feed my family does not give anyone the right to steal my vehicle and cause my death. Because I was armed the morning of November 18, 2002, a potentially deadly event was stopped and I went home alive. I would have it no other way. Neither should you.

Chapter 2 - Making the Decision

Kathy Jackson

*Florida Title XLVI, 790.10 Improper exhibition of danger-
ous weapons or firearms.—If any person having or carrying any
dirk, sword, sword cane, firearm, electric weapon or device, or
other weapon shall, in the presence of one or more persons, exhibit the same in a rude, careless, angry, or threatening manner, not in necessary self-defense, the person so offending shall
be guilty of a misdemeanor of the first degree, punishable as
provided in s. 775.082 or s. 775.083.*

[1]In Florida, as in other states, it is illegal to brandish or
threaten other people with dangerous weapons. There is one
notable exception, however: it's perfectly legal to display or exhibit a firearm "in necessary self-defense." What this means is
that, contrary to internet public opinion, a person does not *have
to* fire the weapon in order to use it lawfully for self defense. In
most states, if self defense is necessary, displaying the firearm
as a deterrent is within the bounds of the law. That is why Mark
Walters' friend informed him that he hadn't violated any laws
when he displayed his handgun to prevent a physical attack.

1-Much of the material in this chapter is heavily drawn from lectures given in
Massad Ayoob's LFI-1 and Judicious Use of Deadly Force Instructor classes. The
author strongly recommends Ayoob's material for anyone who is serious about
defending themselves while staying upon the right side of the law.

Similar laws are in effect in the majority of states, though not in all states. A quick web search will probably reveal similar language in your own state law.

This common point of confusion is understandable. A person interested in armed self-defense often finds himself walking a narrow ridge between two equally unpleasant alternatives. On one side, there is the risk of responding too soon, with too much force, or with unwarranted violence. Erring in that direction sends the shooter stumbling over the rocky cliffs of the American legal system, where even the smallest action can have huge consequences that affect the entire life. "Better to be tried by twelve ..." as the saying goes, but anyone with an ounce of sense knows that an 8x12 cell isn't much of a life. On the other side of the ridge lies the stony valley of death or severe injury caused by responding too slowly – or by not responding at all – to a lethal force attack.

Of the two dangers, most people rightly fear death more than they fear the tender ministrations of the legal system. And that's as it should be, but that doesn't mean that one should be uninformed about or unwilling to consider the laws which affect an armed citizen. Quite the contrary! The only true victory in a dangerous encounter is to walk away with all of your life intact: your ability to breathe, your good health, your family's safety, and your own freedom. Anything else is a loss.

For this and many other reasons, those who are interested in self-defense should be knowledgeable about the laws which affect them. One good place to start is with an online search. Stop by www.handgunlaw.us or www.usacarry.org for handy, direct links to state and local laws. Visit www.gunlaws.com, author

Alan Korwin's well-organized site, which provides well-written web and print legal resources for every state in the union.

For those who prefer to do their research on bound paper, there are many options. At the federal level, Korwin's *Gun Laws of America*[2] supplies an excellent overview of national gun laws, while his state gun-law series gives a good picture of the law in several individual states. Kevin L. Jamison, a Missouri lawyer and columnist for *Concealed Carry Magazine*, penned an excellent in-depth book for Missouri residents: *Missouri Weapons and Self-Defense Law*[3]. Longtime gun-rights journalist Dave Workman did a similar (but much less in-depth) work for Washington residents: *Washington State Gun Rights and Responsibilities*[4]. In Florida, the reference book of choice is the incredibly detailed *Florida Firearms – Law, Use, and Ownership*[5] by Jon Gutmacher. Similar works are available in every one of the fifty states, and are worth seeking out.

In addition to these, on every gun owner's bookshelf should be a copy of Massad Ayoob's classic *In the Gravest Extreme*[6]. This volume (originally published in 1980 and never updated) speaks to the timeless principles which build the foundation for all defense laws common to western civilization. It provides an absolutely indispensable understanding of how the law views the armed citizen who defends innocent life with deadly force,

2-Alan Korwin, *Gun Laws of America,* Bloomfield Press 2005. Order from Bloomfield Press, 4848 E. Cactus, #505-440, Scottsdale, AZ 85254, or online from www.gunlaws.com

3-Kevin L. Jamison, *Missouri Weapons and Self Defense Law,* Merril Press 2003. Order from 2614 NE 56th Terrace, Gladstone, MO 64119-2311or online from www.kljamisonlaw.com

4-Dave Workman, *Washington State Gun Rights and Responsibilities*, D&D Enterprises. Order from D&D Enterprises, P.O. Box 1638, North Bend, WA 98045 or online from www.danddgunleather.com

5-Jon H. Gutmacher, Esq., *Florida Firearms – Law, Use, and Ownership,* Warlord Publishing. Order from publisher at 200 N. Thornton Ave., Orlando, FL 32801 or online from www.floridafirearmslaw.com

6-Massad F. Ayoob, *In the Gravest Extreme: the Role of the Firearm in Personal Protection*. Police Bookshelf 1980. Order from Police Bookshelf, PO Box 122, Concord, NH 03302 or online at www.Ayoob.com

and supplies some commonsense measures an intelligent person can take which greatly reduce the chances of legal trouble following a life-threatening encounter.

Although the specific laws about deadly force are different from one state to the next, in the United States there is one fairly uniform standard on using deadly force which, if followed, will keep you within the law no matter where you live. This standard has its roots in common law and has been used as a benchmark in law enforcement training for many, many years. It applies whether you are at home or in public, no matter what method your attacker uses to try to do you harm. As long as your response to his actions falls entirely within this standard, your legal position will be very strong.

The Basic Standard:

You may legally use deadly force only when there is an *immediate and otherwise unavoidable danger of death or grave bodily harm to the innocent.*

In order to meet this basic rule, you must be able to convince a jury that you (or the person you defended) were an innocent party, and that you were in immediate and *otherwise unavoidable* danger of death or grave bodily harm.

Meeting the *immediate* part of the standard isn't too difficult. You fight back only when the danger is actually present, not when it *might* be present sometime in the future or *was* present sometime in the past. If someone threatens to kill you tomorrow, you don't gun him down today; you get a restraining order and make sure he can't find you tomorrow. If someone attacks you and then runs off, you don't shoot him in the backside no matter how badly you want to. If someone leaves the scene to get a weapon, you get out of Dodge as quickly as you can so you aren't there when he gets back. You don't use deadly force unless the danger of getting killed or maimed is right then and right there. The danger must be present at the very moment you pull the trigger.

Since you're a smart person, if you could have figured out another way to avoid the danger you would have done it. If you were in public, you probably tried to walk away or disengage. In your own home, you probably tried getting behind furniture, or barring the door, or even leaving the house.[7] If time permitted, you called 911. Your actions must show that shooting the attacker was the absolute last thing on your list of things you wanted to do. That is how you meet the otherwise unavoidable part of the standard. The citizen who acts with lethal force must always be able to show that it was a last resort under the circumstances. It's important to note, however, that even in states where there is a "duty to retreat" from an assailant, retreat is ***never*** required unless it can be accomplished in complete safety to oneself and other persons. You need not try to outrun a bullet, or throw your helpless children to the attacking wolves.

Showing that you were the *innocent* party is also fairly straightforward in most cases. If you don't habitually get into bar brawls or yell at other people, if you've learned to deal with beggars by saying no and walking away, if you don't get involved in road-rage incidents – all of these are commonsense things your mother probably told you, and although mom probably didn't know it she was giving you sound legal advice. If you did not willingly participate in an altercation or egg it on, the court will see that you were an innocent party.

7-Leaving the house is not legally necessary in any state the author is aware of, but in some circumstances it might be a good practical tactic.

But how can you know and prove that the situation you were in was truly life-threatening, and really involved a danger of grave bodily harm or even death?

Police are trained to answer this question by looking for three basic elements that must be present before they may use lethal force. These three elements are called *Ability, Opportunity*, and *Jeopardy* (often abbreviated to AOJ, or referred to as the "AOJ triad"). When these three things are present, any reasonable person would believe that a life was in danger, so the defendant's legal position is very strong. But if one of the elements is missing, the defendant may have a hard time convincing a jury that shooting the attacker was really necessary.[8]

Ability, Opportunity, Jeopardy

Important Definitions
Ability means that the other person has the power to kill or to cripple you.
Opportunity means that the circumstances are such that the other person would be able to use his ability against you.
Jeopardy means that the other person's actions or words provide you with a reasonably-perceived belief that he intends to kill you or cripple you.

It is important to realize that any two of these elements may be present in a lot of ordinary interactions. The presence of only two elements does not justify using deadly force. This isn't as complicated as it sounds, and it is mostly just hard common sense.

8-See "Defending the Self-Defense Case" by Lisa J. Steele, in the March 2007 issue of the National Association of Criminal Defense Lawyers' journal, the Champion.

An example of A & O, but not J: a strong young man with a baseball bat (ability) is standing within a few feet of a man in a wheelchair (opportunity). Unless the young man either verbally or physically threatens to assault the other man, jeopardy is not present.

An example of O & J, but not A: a very irate little girl says, "I hate you! I'm going to kill you!" (jeopardy). She is standing right next to you, close enough to hit you with every ounce of her strength (opportunity). But she's only a little girl, and she doesn't have any weapons. Ability is not present.

An example of A & J, but not O: a small female has just testified in court against a male criminal who has been trained as a martial artist and who is physically much bigger and stronger than she is (ability). As the guilty verdict is read, the criminal rages to his feet and begins shouting and threatening to kill her right then and there (jeopardy). But he is restrained by hand-cuffs and by the bailiffs. Opportunity is not present.

Now that we have defined our terms and have seen the simple overview, let's examine each of the individual elements more closely.

Ability

The power to kill or cripple another human being can be represented by a lot of different things. Most often, it is represented by a weapon of some sort: a gun, a knife, a tire iron or club, or even some improvised weapon like a screwdriver or a metal chain. This isn't a complete list, of course. The number of items that could be used as deadly weapons is nearly infinite, and they all represent ability. But *ability* can be present even when a weapon is not.

If a weapon is not present, ability may be represented by something the courts call *disparity of force*. This is just a fancy phrase that means the fight would be so radically unfair and so unevenly matched that any reasonable bystander would agree that one of the participants could kill or permanently damage the other person even without a weapon. Disparity of force is figured out on a case-by-case basis, taking in the entire set of circumstances. Generally speaking, disparity exists:

- When a strong young person attacks a really old person
- When three or more people attack one person
- When an adult attacks a child
- When a healthy person attacks someone who is handicapped
- When a known, skilled martial artist attacks someone who is not a martial artist
- When one participant has become so badly injured that he is unable to physically defend himself from a continued violent assault
- When a man attacks a woman

Let me repeat that last point for emphasis: *when an unarmed man attacks a woman, the courts generally recognize that disparity of force is present*. This means that if a woman is attacked even by an unarmed man, she may generally assume that ability exists. A male attacker who goes after a female victim does not have to display a weapon in order to be a deadly threat to her. A woman who is attacked may reasonably believe that even an unarmed male possesses the power to kill her or to severely injure her.[9]

9-It is particularly important that women understand this point as it relates to sexual assault. Almost any unarmed adult male can kill or seriously injure an adult

Opportunity

Opportunity means that the total circumstances are such that the other person would be able to use his ability to maim or kill you. It includes, but is not limited to, questions such as how close he is to where you are, what objects might be between you and him, whether you have a readily-available means of stopping him from reaching you, and what he is armed with if he is armed at all.

When opportunity is present, a person armed with a gun will be within shooting distance (which can be quite far away, depending upon the particular firearm, and especially if there is no readily-available cover for the intended victims to shelter behind). If he is armed with a blade or an impact weapon, he will be room distance from you or closer, with no impediments between you. He will be close enough to kill you with whatever weapon he has, or with his bare hands. And there will be nothing in the environment to prevent him from doing so.

Probably the most important thing to note about opportunity is that if the other person is armed with an impact weapon or a blade, they can possess the element of opportunity even if they are on the other side of an average household room. This is because an average adult human being can cover 21 feet of distance in about 1.5 seconds or a little less. If you have practiced on the range with a timer, you know that is just barely enough time to draw your gun from concealment and get one good shot downrange. These time frames show that an attacker armed with

female using only his bare hands (ability); in order to complete the rape, the man must be close enough to kill or cripple (opportunity); and even if the rapist never says a word to his intended victim, the implicit threat of death or grave injury if the intended victim does not comply is part of what defines the crime of rape (jeopardy). This means that in most situations, it is legal for a woman to use a firearm to defend herself against a man who attempts to commit forcible rape, even if he is unarmed.

an impact weapon can swarm you and kill you before you are able to draw your gun, unless you begin the defensive process before he covers that distance.[10]

Jeopardy

Jeopardy – sometimes called *manifest intent* – is the most difficult of the three elements to articulate, and often the most difficult to prove in court. The reason for this is that human beings are not mind readers. You cannot *know*, beyond any shadow of a doubt, what another person is thinking and what he intends to do. You can only reasonably perceive his intentions based upon his actions and his words.

Simple fear isn't enough to establish that jeopardy is present. Someone who "looks menacing" may in fact be an innocent person with unfortunate facial features. Being afraid of what someone *might* do, when they have not given any real indication that they *will* do it, does not establish jeopardy.

As with the other two elements, jeopardy is really based on the entire set of surrounding circumstances. The jury will be instructed to ask themselves whether a reasonable and prudent person, knowing exactly what you knew at that moment (and no more!), would have come to the same conclusion you did. Would a reasonable and prudent person have believed that your attacker meant to use his ability to kill or cripple you? Was your decision that the person was a threat based upon simple fear, or

---

10-From a legal perspective, you must be able to document that you knew this before the attack, however. One way to do this is to take a class which includes "the Tueller Drill," named after its creator, Dennis Tueller. Be sure to take dated notes, and to keep those notes in a secure place in case you ever need to authenticate your knowledge of the danger posed by an attacker at these distances. In the absence of a class, you may be able to document your knowledge by purchasing the *Surviving Edged Weapons* video made by Calibre Press (a gory but instructional film intended for police officers in training), or by viewing *How Close Is Too Close?* by Dennis Tueller and Massad Ayoob. Both are available from Police Bookshelf, PO Box 122, Concord, NH 03302 or online at www.Ayoob.com. The day you watch the video, sign and date the video jacket for later reference.

did his actions and/or words give you a reasonable perception that he intended to kill you? What did the other person say or do, what physical motions did he make, which convinced you that he meant to do you harm?

Jeopardy does not necessarily require a clear verbal statement that the other person is trying to kill or cripple you, and words alone are not enough to establish it. Some attacks might include a spoken threat ("I'm going to kill you!" or "See this knife? I'm gonna cut your throat..."). These types of verbal statements, along with a related physical motion, may be used to help establish jeopardy. But jeopardy can be present even when the other person does not say a single word. For example, an intruder who climbs in through a bedroom window, brandishes a knife, and advances toward you may be showing that he intends to violently attack you with a deadly weapon. Jeopardy would be present because the intruder's physical actions clearly demonstrate his probable intent.

Jeopardy can be present even if the other person later says he was "just joking," or if it turns out the gun or knife he was threatening you with was nothing but a toy. Remember, the jury will be instructed to ask themselves whether a reasonable and prudent person, knowing exactly what you knew at the time (and no more!) would have come to the same conclusion you did. If the person was acting in such a way that anyone with a lick of sense would have believed he really did intend to maim or kill you, then jeopardy did in fact exist no matter what other facts might come to light after the dust settles.

So that's the legal reality of armed self defense: you may legally use deadly force when there is an *immediate and otherwise unavoidable danger of death or grave bodily harm to the innocent.* The individual elements that create this standard include some very complex legal doctrines, but once the key concepts are understood, the bottom line is surprisingly commonsense: you may legally use deadly force if you realistically believe your life is in imminent danger and there is no other reasonable action you can take to avoid that danger.

The Moral Dilemma

The knowledge that you are standing on firm legal ground provides an important element of self-confidence when dealing with an assailant. And yet, armed with that knowledge, some citizens remain reluctant to react with ultimate force even in situations where there is clearly no other choice but to be killed. This reluctance to act can often be traced to moral qualms and ethical dilemmas.

In simplest form, this reluctance can be summed up in a single, scornful accusation from an outsider: "It'll just get taken away from you and used against you." If such an accusation is more likely to be aimed at women than men, that would be because there's a perception in our society that women are the keepers of our social conscience: more tender of feeling, more delicate of conscience, more reluctant to make the hard choice. But when life and death are on the line, men are no less likely than women to suffer from a moral crisis. The accusation may be annoying, but it is based upon an important foundational truth: If you pull out a gun and are not morally and emotionally prepared to use it if necessary, you are indeed at risk for a gun grab or worse.

A lot of gun owners swim in a sea of euphemisms; I just did it myself. "Use it if necessary" avoids the blunter but more honest, "to kill another human being." If speaking bluntly about the use of our defensive firearms doesn't come easily to most of us, how much easier would the deed itself be? Socially, psychologically, and emotionally, few people are able to consider unwaveringly the full implications of using a deadly weapon for self defense.

"A very large percentage of people who carry a concealed handgun do not carry it as a weapon. They carry it as a good luck charm. They think of it as a magic talisman that wards off evil, or as a rabbit's foot," says firearms instructor Tom Givens. But the mere presence of the gun is no magic bullet. Without the mental willingness to use the gun in the final extreme, its usefulness is strictly limited.

Many people who purchase a gun do so because they had some sort of an unpleasant incident, an encounter which created in them an awareness of vulnerability and a determination not to let it happen again. This isn't universal by any means, but it is a common first step. But plenty of people encounter violence every day, and they don't decide to fight back next time. They don't decide to go armed. So the journey to determined self defense might begin with an awareness of vulnerability, but it does not end there.

Some bedrock questions to consider during the journey: what are you willing to fight for? What is so important to you that you would be willing to do whatever it takes to defend it? Is there anything? A lot of people say no to this question, straight up. *Nothing* is worth taking another human's life, they say. But a little probing might give a different answer.

"I wouldn't fight back to save my own life," a friend of mine once confessed, "but if someone tried to touch one of my babies, *well...!*" This isn't an uncommon sentiment, and a lot of parents who are otherwise passively unwilling to fight admit that they would do literally anything to protect their children's lives. Taking it a step further, some people become willing to fight for their own lives the day they realize that their kids would be harmed by growing up without a parent. For Mark Walters, getting home to his infant daughter was a strong motivator.

Nor is this dynamic unique to those who have children. One woman of my acquaintance first became willing to use a gun simply because she heard a news story wherein an intruder killed the family dogs before attacking the female homeowner. My friend hadn't previously been willing to fight on her own behalf, but realized she would fight to protect her beloved pets.

Self-defense instructor Tony Blauer[11] takes this common trait and runs with it in his tapes and seminars. Blauer suggests that his students make a list of things they would lose if they did *not* fight back, things which are already present in the student's life, which are personal to each student, and about which the student is passionate. With these powerful personal symbols, students give themselves permission to fight back.

Religious people often face more daunting hurdles on their road to fighting back. From the sacredness of all life in some devotional traditions to the staunch pacifism of others, from 'thou shalt not kill' in Judaism to 'turn the other cheek' in Christendom, from the ahimsa of Hinduism to the dharma of Buddhism, most religions contain at least some elements that could be at odds with lethal self-defense. Overcoming the qualms caused by these teachings can take time, diligent study, and much soul-searching.

11-Blauer Tactical Systems USA, LLC. 476 Viking Drive #101, Virginia Beach, VA 23452. (877) 773-2748. www.tonyblauer.com

Some religious difficulties are simply the result of misunderstandings. While most Christians and Jews have heard, "Thou shalt not kill," for example, only a relative few know that the Hebrew word often translated as "kill," would more properly be translated "murder" by most scholars. Many similar questions can be cleared up by discussion with a more knowledgeable friend, or with a religious leader.[12] Sometimes, the answers will be surprising. When a little girl asked the Dalai Lama a question about school violence, for instance, the Dalai Lama told her "it would be reasonable to shoot back with your own gun" in some situations.[13]

Occasionally, a deeply spiritual person will sense a conflict between trusting God and defending one's own life. Further thought might show that trusting God to protect one's life doesn't have to be at odds with defending oneself – not any more than working for and then preparing one's own meals is at odds with trusting Him to provide one's daily bread. Christians believe that God created human beings as tool-users with creative minds, in a universe governed by cause and effect, in a world where actions have consequences. This being the case, it seems less than faithful for a believer to shun tools, reject thoughtful preparation, and avoid putting forth any personal effort. As Galileo Galilei put it, "I do not feel obliged to believe that the same God who has endowed us with sense, reason, and intellect has intended us to forego their use."

Does even a murderer or a child molester or a rapist deserve to be killed for his actions? Such a question can haunt the ethical

12-For Christians, one place to begin this study might be with Charl Van Wyk's book *Shooting Back: The Right and Duty of Self-Defence* (Christian Liberty Books, 2001), which makes the case for armed self-defense from a Christian perspective.
13-Reported in the Seattle Times, May 15, 2001, by Hal Bernton.

person. But perhaps a more perceptive question would be, "*Who decided* that this conflict was worth a human life?" When an assailant raises a deadly weapon toward an innocent person, the assailant has already made the most important choice of the day: he has decided that someone is going to die. The only decision left for anyone else to make is whether the person who dies that day will be an innocent victim, or one of society's predators.

In the final analysis, each person's journey on the road to armed self-defense is intensely personal. After all, the decision that your own life is worth defending, even if it comes at the cost of killing another human being, cuts right through the heart of some very personal territory which encompasses deeply held moral, ethical, and religious beliefs. Ultimately, those who own defensive firearms must decide for themselves where their own boundary lines lie. Each individual must decide alone what it will take for them to say to an attacker, "Not me. Not mine. Not today."

Chapter 3 - The Political Bravery of Michael DeBose

Mark Walters

I remember reading the original article through a link to the *Cleveland Plain Dealer* found on a website run by Buckeye Firearms Association, one of the nation's most effective pro-gun grassroots organizations. As the story went, Mr. Michael DeBose was out taking a walk for his health one beautiful afternoon during the summer of 2007 when he was accosted by three thugs. Mr. DeBose was able to escape being killed that afternoon because his wife and neighbors heard his screams for help. He is lucky to be alive today and he knows it.

What made that newspaper column so fascinating is the fact that Mr. DeBose is not your ordinary Ohio citizen. He is better known as Ohio State Representative Michael DeBose, a Democrat representing Ohio's District 12 in Cleveland with 117,000 constituents.

Ohio had been embroiled in a political battle for concealed carry of weapons (CCW) rights for many years under turncoat Republican governor Taft who refused to sign CCW legislation into law, and Representative DeBose was openly on the record as opposing the legislation. In fact, he voted against it twice in the legislature. Ohio eventually passed "shall issue" carry and it went into effect statewide in April of 2006.

The *Cleveland Plain Dealer*, a rabidly anti-gun newspaper that regularly publishes the names and addresses of law abiding citizens who receive Ohio CCW permits, was reporting that Representative DeBose was now going on record as having changed his mind. DeBose was seeking the protection Ohio's new law afforded its citizens – the very law he voted against two times.

I placed a call to Representative DeBose's office seeking an interview and identifying myself as a columnist for *Concealed Carry Magazine*. Much to my surprise, I received a call back from him only hours later. After a brief discussion, Representative Debose agreed to be interviewed for my column, and he and I developed a quick rapport during our subsequent conversations. What follows is a fascinating discussion with him regarding a frightening, life altering experience that gave him the bravery to stand up for what he knows is right.

Mark Walters: Mr. DeBose, welcome and thank you very much for taking time out of your very busy schedule to talk with us tonight, sir.

Rep. DeBose: Thank you for having me.

Mark Walters: Representative DeBose, can you tell the readers what district you represent and how long you've represented your constituents?

Rep. DeBose: I represent District 12 in Ohio, the southeast side of Cleveland. I represent 117,000 residents. I've represented them for approximately seven years. This is my third term. I have one more term left.

Mark Walters: Sir, obviously violent crime is of the utmost concern to all Americans. The *Cleveland Plain Dealer* recently reported that you yourself were a victim of a violent attack. Sir, can you tell us in your own words what happened that day?

Rep. DeBose: I was taking a walk from my house to the corner. I live six houses from the corner and I had just come back from Columbus where we were in session. We had just passed some important pieces of legislation. As I walked to the corner, I had no incidents. When I turned around to walk back home I was three houses from the corner. These houses are about 40 feet away from each other – but a car pulled up with a loud muffler and the driver stays in the car. Two guys get out of the passenger side, one tall, one short. The tall one had braids in his hair. He had a gun.

They started to come at me and I was about 50 to 100 feet away from them. At that point, I started to run. I knew they were up to no good so I backed up and then I started to run. I was yelling, hollering and screaming. I was yelling for my neighbor. I was yelling for my wife. I was yelling for my daughter. My wife and my daughter came outside. The short one, he heard me yelling and screaming. Other people did, too. So, he ran back to the car and they took off, they being the driver and the short one.

The tall one with the gun – he kept coming after me. Then my wife came out and she was very visible. I ran up on my neighbor's porch and I started banging on her door and ringing the doorbell. Lights started coming on. Then he, being the one with the gun, turns around and runs up the street but the car was gone. So the driver must have looked in the mirror, saw him and then they made a U-turn, picked him up and then they came up the street. I could've been hurt. I could've been killed. I could've been injured. I would not be here to see my grandchildren. I might not be here to enjoy my wife. There's no need to do that.

Mark Walters: Obviously, it was unbelievably frightening.

Rep. DeBose: Yes, it was. It was something that – it was a life altering experience.

Mark Walters: Was your wife in any danger at the time she saw the criminals attacking you, or was she responsible in your mind for helping to frighten them off?

Rep. DeBose: Well, she helped frighten them away. I don't think she was in danger. She saved my life because there's no telling what these guys would've done. Now you give them your money, your jewelry, your watches and they still kill you.

Mark Walters: Life has certainly changed on the streets in America today, sir. It's unfortunate but the gun debate that's raged across this country has widely been portrayed on the national level as a political debate between liberal Democrats and conservative Republicans. I, as a conservative leaning writer admit that I myself have politicized this debate. After hearing your story, sir, I felt it incredibly important that our readers hear from you. Our readers know that violent crime affects all walks of life and does not discriminate between political opinions in any way. What happened to you is truly a human story, not a political one. Can you tell us how this may have changed your views since that attack occurred?

Rep. DeBose: To be honest with you, I'm not promoting guns, quite honestly. I voted against concealed carry twice but when this happened – someone points a gun at you and you feel hopeless and helpless and you want some way to defend yourself and your family – then your perspective changes. Any person who has a gun pulled on them has walked in my shoes. Quite frankly I don't want to experience that again. I don't want them to either. It changed my views in that I'm only dealing with me. I can't tell other people what to do and I'm not encouraging other people to do something that I'm doing. I'm only dealing with myself. It's in my best interest to get a gun.

Mark Walters: Sir, as you probably now know, making the decision to carry a firearm for self-defense is a very personal one. As an elected public official your personal decision to do so has been made public by the *Cleveland Plain Dealer*. What are your thoughts on the publicity that you've received? Have you received any negative publicity?

Rep. DeBose: I've received some and I've received some support – but I've got more support than negative publicity. I got hammered in the papers. In Sunday's paper about carrying a concealed weapon, there were three letters to the editor that disagree with me carrying a weapon. I got no letters that supported me. I know that letters came in to support me but they were all anti-gun letters. My wife has picked her application up, she's filled it out and she'll be turning it in.

Mark Walters: Have you taken the class in Ohio yet?

Rep. DeBose: No, I haven't taken the classes yet. We haven't taken them yet.

Mark Walters: So you are going to follow through and pick up your concealed carry permit for both you and your wife?

Rep. DeBose: Yes. Other people have inquired about it, and to be honest with you, I was told by a reporter that he was given names and numbers of people that want to offer training for myself and my wife and anybody else that I wanted to bring. So, I've been telling people that, and I've been offering that service to them. There's more interest out there than I actually thought.

Mark Walters: That's fantastic that you've made that decision. Our organization obviously supports you. The USCCA[1] stresses the vital importance of firearms training above and beyond that required by our respective states to receive the permit. Not only do we feel that it promotes gun safety, but it's also a fun activity. The shooting sports

1-United States Concealed Carry Association, N173W21298 Northwest Passage Way, Jackson WI 53037. (877) 677-1919. www.usconcealedcarry.com

are enjoyed by millions of people across the country. Would you consider taking any additional training above and beyond what the state of Ohio requires?

Rep. DeBose: Yes. That's mandatory. I want to become proficient in not only the firing of a firearm but the handling of it and the knowledge of it in terms of when to use it, when not to use it, how to store it and make it safe because my wife will probably get hers before I get mine. I want her to be comfortable with how to handle it in terms of how to carry it and when to pull it because a gun is something when you pull it you have to use it. It's not something to play with.

Mark Walters: Sir, I want to thank you very much for your time today. I really appreciate your honesty and your candor in discussing what was a violent and very frightening incident. Are there any additional thoughts or any points that you would like to make to our readers and members?

Rep. DeBose: I would like people to understand one thing. Don't judge people by what they do or what they don't do. Until you've walked in that person's shoes, you don't understand what brought them to that decision. This decision has been a personal one. I'm not after anyone to be a copycat and I'm not going around starting trouble with a gun. I'm not going around asking people to get out of my way and like I'm some type of bully. The only thing I'm saying is that you have to have an equalizer on the street. These streets are dangerous. There are killers and they're equal opportunity murderers. These people are mean-spirited and they're evil. You have to have a way to get their attention to let them know that you're not playing with them. Bottom line is, personally I'm not taking it anymore. We have to take our streets back. We have to take our neighborhoods back. I'm not moving. I'm not going to leave the area. I'm not going to run and I'm not going to stop taking my walks because I need the exercise. So I'm going to continue to do what I was doing and nobody's going to stop me from doing it.

Mark Walters: If there is anything that you need or any questions that you have regarding continued training, please feel free to let us know and we will support you. Representative DeBose, I want to thank you very much for your valuable time today and for allowing me to bring this story to our readers.

Rep. DeBose: Okay. Thank you very much for having me.

During my subsequent conversations with Representative DeBose, he asked me if I could assist him with his firearm training class. I had made a list of some folks in Ohio for him to contact when he told me that Mr. Jim Irvine of Buckeye Firearms Association[2] had contacted him. Jim and I spoke shortly after that conversation and I informed him of my interview with Representative DeBose.

Through the dedication and hard work of many people, Jim was able to put together the necessary training for Representative DeBose and a group of his associates, friends and neighbors. A special thanks goes out to Mr. Ken Hanson and Mr. Jim Wilson of Buckeye Firearms Association and Mr. Keith Campbell of Commence Firearms Training Academy.

I would also like to thank Peter Pi and Elaine Pi of CorBon Ammunition. I had contacted several ammunition manufacturers seeking a donation for the large quantity of ammunition that the class would require and Peter and Elaine were most gracious in supplying several thousand high-quality rounds of various calibers used during the training class. Thanks to all of you!

These fine, dedicated folks donated their valuable time and made sure that Representative DeBose, his wife and associates

2-Buckeye Firearms Association, 15 West Winter Street, Delaware, Ohio 43015. www.buckeyefirearms.org

received the finest firearm training that the state of Ohio has to offer.

So what makes this story so vitally important? I can tell you that Representative DeBose and I developed a unique friendship since this interview occurred, and my perspective on some things has changed. First, this is not a political story and I tried very hard to keep politics out of the conversation. The thugs who attacked Michael DeBose did not care who he votes for, whether he is a Democrat or a Republican or what color his skin is. The fact that he is a politician was never known to the animals who tried to deprive him of his liberties.

What matters here is the human side of this story, that crime crosses all walks of life and is a potential threat to everyone. The fact that the major media has largely portrayed guns as a Democrat vs. Republican issue seems to leave behind the importance of the human side of the debate. Yes, it's true that a general distinction can be made between the major political parties when it comes to guns and the right to keep and bear arms, but by doing so we close our eyes to the larger, more important picture.

Violent crime is a personal, human story that crosses all party lines and thanks to my conversations with Representative Michael DeBose, I for one will be more careful when I catch myself painting the canvas of my word processor with a broad brush from now on.

Representative DeBose and his wife have since applied for and received their Ohio CCW licenses.

Chapter 4 - What are the Odds?

Kathy Jackson

As Rep. DeBose discovered, a criminal attack rarely happens when the intended victim is expecting it. In fact, if the criminal believes you are expecting him to attack and are prepared to cope with it, he's very likely to take his "business" elsewhere.

Nevertheless, one of the arguments people often use against regular, every day concealed carry comes in the form of a simple question: "What are the odds?"

This isn't an easy question to answer, in part because of the limitations of statistics which are never complete. It's also difficult to answer because dry numbers, no matter how dramatically those numbers might make the case, carry little weight to someone who feels safe in their home, neighborhood, and community. Why should someone put up with all the hassle and social disapproval of carrying a deadly weapon when they don't feel threatened in the first place?

But let's start with those statistics nevertheless. The numbers are here to show the coldly logical that yes, it *can* happen to you.[1]

In 2007, throughout the United States, there was

- a violent crime every 22.4 seconds.

1-Statistics taken from the FBI's Uniform Crime Reports "Crime Clock," found online at http://www.fbi.gov/ucr/ucr.htm. Accessed 12/13/2008.

- a murder every 31 minutes.
- a forcible rape every 5.8 minutes.
- a robbery every 1.2 minutes.
- an aggravated assault every 36.8 seconds.
- a property crime every 3.2 seconds.
- a burglary every 14.5 seconds.

As bad as these numbers sound, they actually reflect a *falling* crime rate, not a rising one.

But we needn't resort to numbers in order to make the most compelling case of all. Here it is: every single innocent victim who has ever been attacked, anywhere or anywhen, was not expecting that attack to happen. If they had been expecting it, they would not have been there in the first place!

Blood running in the streets!
The politics of concealed carry

During the decades between 1980 and the present, many states passed "shall issue" laws authorizing concealed carry by ordinary citizens. In states with a shall-issue law, the citizen who wishes to carry a concealed firearm must meet specific requirements defined by law; if a citizen meets the requirements, the state "shall issue" a permit. In contrast to this, a few holdout states (two as of this writing) forbid citizens to carry under any circumstances whatsoever; two allow unrestricted and unlicensed carry by any citizen; and the remainder have "may issue" laws which allow an individual bureaucrat or politician to make the final decision whether to issue a permit to citizens who wish to carry concealed – a decision all too often based merely on the bureaucrat's whim and personal prejudices, or upon whether the applicant has recently contributed to a campaign fund.[2]

2-This isn't sarcasm or hyperbole; it's the literal truth. For more information, see *"Gun Laws Breed Corruption,"* by Dr. Michael S. Brown, published online

As they were being passed, shall-issue laws were, almost without exception, hotly contested and vigorously debated in state houses across the country. Many of the bills which would authorize concealed carry were rejected time and again before finally they were finally passed into law. In every state, the argument anti-gun people most often used against them became a rallying cry: "There will be blood running in the streets!"

This isn't true, of course. Hasn't happened. In Florida, for instance, the number of concealed carry permit holders involved in crime was consistently around 0.02 percent of all carry permit holders in the decade after Florida's right-to-carry law went into effect in 1988.[3] In Texas, where shall-issue carry laws began in 1996, an analysis of arrest data for Texas concealed handgun licensees that was performed on data from the subsequent five years found that Texans *without* carry permits were 7.5 to 7.7 times more likely to be arrested for violent crimes than were Texans *with* carry permits. Of the few permit holders who were arrested, only 26 percent were later convicted of the crimes for which they were arrested; and of the permit holders who were arrested for violent crimes, 44 percent were cleared. No male Texas CHL holder was arrested for negligent manslaughter during the 1996 through 2000 period, nor was any female Texas CHL holder arrested for negligent manslaughter, rape, or robbery.[4]

---

at http://www.enterstageright.com/archive/articles/0102/0102gunlaws.htm and accessed 12/13/2008. See also "*Shall Issue: the New Wave of Concealed Handgun Permit Laws*" (especially the section titled "Modern Discretionary Permits"), by Dave Kopel and Clayton E. Cramer, published online at http://www.i2i.org/main/article.php?article_id=643 and accessed 12/13/2008.
3-See *GunFacts 5.1* (available online through www.gunfacts.info), which references a 1998 Florida Department of Justice study.
4-*An Analysis Of The Arrest Rate Of Texas Concealed Handgun License Holders As Compared To The Arrest Rate Of The Entire Texas Population 1996 - 1998, Revised to include 1999 and 2000 data*, by William E. Sturdevant, PE. Accessed online at http://www.txchia.org/sturdevant2000.htm on 12/13/2008.

If merely obtaining a carry permit transformed otherwise law-abiding citizens into bloodthirsty predators (as the proponents of the "blood running in the streets" models would have us believe), those statistics would look very different indeed. Rather, the evidence shows that citizens who go through the process to obtain permission to carry legal firearms are less violent than their peers, less likely to get into trouble with the law, and more likely to stay out of trouble.

Rep. DeBose found himself caught in the midst of one of these controversies during the fight to legalize concealed carry in Ohio. And – once his emotions were swayed by a personal event – he began to understand *why* an ordinary, innocent person might want a gun in everyday circumstances. He was finally able to accept the counterintuitive but accurate statistics that show us that violent crime does not increase in areas where gun ownership increases.

It's understandable that an ordinary person might dislike firearms and be repulsed by the idea of shooting a violent attacker. Such compassionate folks often resort to the bumper-sticker slogan, "Imagine a world without guns!" Such a world, they reason, would be full of kindhearted souls with humanitarian goals, where justice is widely practiced and violence nonexistent.

Reality isn't quite so pretty. As Dave Kopel, Paul Gallant, and Joanne Eisen wrote in *National Review*,

> *To imagine a world with no guns is to imagine a world in which the strong rule the weak, in which women are dominated by men, and in which minorities are easily abused or mass-murdered by majorities. Practically speaking, a firearm is the only weapon that allows a weaker person to defend him-*

self from a larger, stronger group of attackers, and to do so at a distance.

In short, to imagine a world without guns is to imagine the return of the Dark Ages.

Paranoid vs prepared

Probably every person who has ever applied for a carry permit has faced the accusation of paranoia from someone who does not understand. Whether it's a loved one, a friend or acquaintance, or simply some dude on the internet, the accusation can sting, and cause the thoughtful person to take a step back. "*Am I being paranoid?*" the prospective permit holder wonders. "Or does getting a carry permit simply mean I wish to be prepared to cope if something bad happens?"

It's interesting how common this perception is, but it's not terribly surprising. We've seen it in other areas too. For instance, some of my early childhood memories involve riding in cars which were not equipped with either seat belts or air bags. Air bags hadn't been invented yet. Seat belts had, but nobody used them. By the time I was ten or eleven years old, my family had begun to wear our seat belts, though not always. Around that time, I can vividly remember getting into a car with a friend's family. As I reached to buckle my seat belt, my friend's dad swung his head around to look at me and said, "Good grief! You don't need to wear that thing. I'm a good driver and we're just going to the store." Plainly evident in his voice and manner was the accusation that I was being *paranoid*, unnecessarily worried about a non-existent threat. Today, of course, everyone wears seat belts – and in most places it's criminal not to do so. What has changed? Not the risk itself. What changed during those decades was the public perception of how acceptable it was to take that risk.

What I'm driving at here is that the accusation of paranoia is one method that people who have rejected a course of action often use to persuade or force others into rejecting it too. It doesn't matter too much what the risk is; someone who doesn't believe the risk is real, or who has chosen to ignore the risk, will always be slightly uncomfortable in the presence of someone who takes the risk seriously. That's why my overweight friend rolls her eyes and complains about "health nuts," and it's why the smoker usually believes that non-smokers overstate the risk of developing lung cancer, and it's why the person who refuses to wear a seat belt or motorcycle helmet is scornful of those who do. Having rejected or denied the risk themselves, these folks simply find it more comfortable to believe that those who respect the risk are "paranoid."

It is true that some folks who carry firearms as private individuals do not have the right mindset for doing so. Some carry it as a magic talisman that will ward off evil just by existing, with the weird idea that as long as they are armed, nothing bad can ever happen to them. Some carry it without understanding the legal and ethical underpinnings of self-defense, and some – sadly! – carry simply because they really are angry at criminals and eager to exact their own brand of justice.

But most of us aren't like that. Most people who carry guns habitually do so simply because we want to be prepared to cope with a criminal crisis, both equipped (with the tools) and prepared (with the mindset) to save our own lives or at least stop the action until the professionals arrive to clean up the mess.

My friend Marko Kloos, who blogs at The Munchkin Wrangler,[5] has another take on this. He writes:

"People who don't like other people carrying guns use the un-likelihood of armed self-defense as an argument against carrying guns. To me, that's like arguing against having a fire extinguisher in your home (or worse, calling owners of such devices "paranoid") because the number of house fires every year is a very small percentage of the total number of dwellings in the country. My counterargument is always that "it's not the odds that bother me, it's what's at stake."

On a related note, I live in a rural area and have a generally low-risk lifestyle. I don't hang out with criminals and my house is an unlikely target for drug seekers. So is my personal risk high enough to justify being armed? If I were carrying simply in order to "feel safe," nope, it's not. I feel plenty safe out here. If I were carrying to lower my risk of attack, again nope. My risk of attack is low, and simply carrying a concealed firearm does not generally lower one's risk of being attacked anyway.[6] But if I were carrying in order to be prepared if trouble struck, well, yes. Yes it is. I don't think my risk of being attacked is particularly high, but if an attack were to happen, my risk of being unable to deal with the situation *without the tools to do so* is very high indeed.

There's another aspect to this whole question of paranoia. Again, Marko Kloos sums it up well, in answer to the question, *why are you so afraid and paranoid that you feel the need to carry a weapon in public?*

This one has always been a head-scratcher for me. Who's

5-See www.munchkinwrangler.blogspot.com. Accessed 12/13/2008.
6-In looking for potential victims, an attacker will not see the concealed firearm and thus the concealed firearm itself provides no deterrent to attack. However, a confident and alert demeanor may create a deterrent effect, and many people find that they are both more confident and more alert while armed.

paranoid: the person who wants to be able to defend himself against the few bad apples in society, or the person who wants to render everybody harmless? Think about what an insult it is to insist on disarming another person. What you're saying to that person is, "I don't trust you until you have no means to harm me." Now that's paranoia.[7]

The bottom line here is that no one but yourself can analyze *your* lifestyle, *your* situation, or what *you* are willing to do in order to defend yourself. An outside accusation of paranoia bears little weight to someone who has evaluated the risks and consequences for themselves, and come to their own conclusions.

Carrying as a default setting

Sooner or later, every person new to concealed carry asks this question, sheepishly, of other people they know who carry. "Would you carry a gun to _____?" they ask. The blank can be filled by any number of things. Would you carry a gun when you go camping? Would you carry to your mom's house? to work? to church? to the movies? to your kids' Little League games?

The question, earnest as it is, always bemuses me somewhat. You see, I don't usually carry a gun *to* anywhere in particular, but I do go places and do things. And I simply carry, wherever I might be.

What I'm getting at is that years ago I made a decision that my default setting would be to carry my gun wherever I went and whatever I was doing. As a result, if I'm ever not carrying, it is because I made a deliberate decision not to do so right then, based upon some specific reason not to do so. So I don't have to

---

7-See http://munchkinwrangler.blogspot.com/2007/03/addendum.html.
Accessed 12/13/2008.

look for reasons why I might want a gun wherever I'm going. I'm taking my gun with me unless I have a good reason not to.

In every situation where I haven't carried in the past couple of years, it's been either specifically illegal, or literally impossible to conceal. Others might have different standards for a good reason not to carry, but that's where my line is.

When I carry, it is never because I think whatever I'm doing is particularly dangerous. If I think something is particularly dangerous, I either don't do it at all, or I find a way to do it more safely – such as going wherever it is during the day instead of at night, or traveling with a friend instead of alone.

A lot of gun owners do the exact opposite. Their default setting is to leave the gun locked up at home. If they carry at all, it's because they made a conscious decision to carry that day – generally because they thought they were doing something particularly dangerous. The only time they carry a gun is when they think they have a specific reason to do so.

People whose default setting is to leave the gun at home often believe that someone who would carry to _____ (fill in your own blank) must be paranoid. After all, there's no specific danger at _____, so why would anyone carry there? That's a common line of thinking among people who own guns but don't carry. But I don't think that way simply because my crystal ball has never been very good. I've noticed that bad things generally happen to me when I'm not expecting it rather than when I am expecting it. For example, I've never been in a *planned* car accident. I've never had a flat tire that I was expecting to get. And the day my middle son was struck by lightning, we sure weren't expecting that to happen!

Don't get me wrong, though. The possibility of becoming paranoid does worry me. You know what I think would cause paranoia for me? Not just getting dressed in the morning and putting my normal stuff in and around my pockets. That can become a regular routine which needn't cause any anxiety. But I suspect that I'd quickly become anxious if I got up in the morning and the first thing I had to think about before I could even get dressed is, "Am I going to go anywhere 'dangerous' today?" To my mind, by the time you've parsed that question, analyzed it from all possible angles, contemplated the criminal statistics for every place you are likely to visit, and mulled over last night's crime news in order to make a simple decision about what to wear, it would be surprising if you didn't begin to develop some kind of twisted thinking. How pleasant would it be to start your day, every day, wondering if your life will be "dangerous enough" today to justify carrying, or thinking about whether or not you might have to kill someone today? No, thank you! That kind of worry isn't for me. Instead, I'll just get dressed in the morning as I usually do, which includes putting on a holstered firearm as a simple routine action rather than as an angst-ridden dissection of potential dangers.

The bottom line is that I choose a low-risk lifestyle, and believe that everywhere I go is relatively free of danger. If it turns out I'm carrying someplace *you* believe is very low risk, what of it? I'm not carrying because I think any particular place is dangerous. I'm carrying because *that's what I do*.

Living the armed lifestyle – some practical tips

If you, too, are convinced that it only makes sense to carry a gun all or nearly all of the time, there are some practical steps you may want to take to prepare.

First and most important: *Get a secure holster*. The importance of this cannot be overstressed. It is unsafe to carry a firearm loose, with an uncovered trigger or an exposed trigger guard. If you prefer to carry the gun in your pocket, get a pocket holster. If you plan to carry the gun in your purse, purchase a purse with a secure internal holster.[8] And if you intend to carry the gun on your belt, get a solid belt and a holster designed to hold the gun securely in place. Don't take chances with your equipment – get the best you can afford and keep it in good repair.

Plan for times and places where you cannot legally carry. If you are unable to legally carry at work, do you intend to lock the gun in your car, and park off the premises? Or will you leave the gun at home instead? If you need to visit the county courthouse, where carry is illegal, how do you plan to secure the gun while you are inside the building? In such situations, a hidden and secure lockbox within the car can be a valuable resource. Furthermore, you may want to ask yourself what other tools you might legally carry in places where guns are prohibited, and get training in how to use those alternative tools.[9]

Learn to anticipate. Even absent legal requirements, there may be times when you will need to remove and secure the gun,

8-Some holster purse sources:
Coronado Leather Company, 1059 Tierra Del Rey, Suite C, Chula Vista, CA 91910. (800) 283-9509. www.coronadoleather.com
Galco International, 2019 West Quail Avenue, Phoenix, Arizona 85027. (800) 874-2526. www.usgalco.com
Ladies Protection, LLC. (661) 993-7160. www.ladiesprotection.com

9-Is an alternative tool "as good as" a firearm? Probably not – unless you DO have the tool, but DON'T have the firearm. The best firearm in the world does you no good at all if it is at home in your safe.

so plan accordingly. For instance, if you are in a group situation and everyone begins talking about jumping into your hostess' swimming pool, you'll know that it will soon be necessary to get the gun off your body and locked up securely before someone throws you in. How are you going to do that? Try to stay a step ahead of the group.

Watch your body language. People tend to notice, in a vague sort of way, when other people are putting out emotional vibes. The stronger the vibes, the more they notice. If you're new to carrying and are not quite sure how you're going to manage this discreetly, remind yourself that you're on the sunny side of the law and have nothing to fear. Don't put off those vibes if you can help it. So don't "sneak." Just matter-of-factly do what you need to do.

Finally, as Breda at the Breda Fallacy blog reminds us:

Carry your gun - it's a lighter burden than regret.[10]

10-See http://thebredafallacy.blogspot.com/2008/11/aim-shoot.html.

Chapter 5 - Get Back in the Car!

Mark Walters

Anyone who has ever been to the North Carolina seashore town of Wilmington can attest to the natural beauty of the area. The sea breezes are cool in the evenings and the weather is mild for most of the winter. The summers, though, can be stifling hot; just ask Steve Murphy.

Like many Americans, Steve's parents had decided to leave the corporate rat race and run a business they could call their own. The Murphys purchased three *Mailboxes, Etc.* franchises located in the Wilmington and Wrightsville Beach area, and were enjoying their new-found freedom from the rigors of corporate life. The entire family pulled together to help the parents run the operation.

July came, and like most young folks in the area, one sunny and stifling hot July afternoon Steve wanted to enjoy some time off near the water. His father had just purchased a new Ford Mustang convertible, and Steve was itching to get it on the streets. Switching vehicles with his dad, he took off, looking to spend some much needed time away from the stress of work.

As Steve remembers it, the early evening of July 10, 2001 was beautiful, clear, and muggy. He recalls turning into his apartment complex drive and passing two people, a male and a female, walking on the sidewalk. "I didn't think anything of them at the time…didn't really even pay any attention to them," he says. Unbeknownst to Steve, the two individuals he had just passed walking through the apartment complex that particular afternoon were *not* there to visit friends.

Pulling into his parking space, Steve exited the Mustang and began putting the top up. Sweating profusely and ready to relax, he walked around the vehicle, opened the trunk and removed his briefcase. He was just about to close the trunk when he heard the words that would change his outlook on life: "Get the f--- in the car!" In an instant, Steve had a .45 caliber semi-automatic handgun pointed directly at his face at point blank range. "I said, get the f--- in the car," he heard again. Standing directly in front of him as he turned towards the building, catching him completely off-guard, was Titus Singleton, a local convicted felon and drug abuser who had been arrested for everything from battery on a female to Peeping Tom. He was not the person Steve would have chosen to meet that hot July afternoon. Accompanying Titus was a female who to this day remains unknown by name. "She was not a dainty woman," Steve told me during our interviews and conversations. "She was quite large. She looked like a linebacker."

Staring down the very large barrel pointing at his face, in shock and disbelief, he remembers feeling anger – anger at himself for being unarmed and leaving his gun in the store. "I was pissed," he told me. "I couldn't believe I didn't have my gun with me. I always carry it with me."

"Drive," yelled Titus, with his muzzle in Steve's face. Not wanting to comply but figuring that it was his only option at that exact moment, Steve decided to do as he was told. Having control of the automobile gave him at least some sense of control of the situation. As he climbed into the driver's seat at gunpoint, he figured he would take them to an ATM, give them what they wanted, and get out of there.

As he drove his dad's car onto Wrightsville Avenue, with a gun stuck in his ribs, he remembered the Sheriff's outpost just blocks away. "No sooner than I thought that, the guy with the gun said, 'Don't even think about driving to the cops.' It was almost like he was reading my mind," Steve remembers ruefully. His four-and-a-half hour odyssey was just beginning.

"I had no idea where we were going. I was forced to drive into an area of town where I had never been before," Steve recalls. Now in unfamiliar territory, behind houses in a neighborhood he had never seen, he was forced out of the car. "I was emptied of the $400 dollars in my pocket. It was money I was supposed to use to have fun that night," Steve told me during our interview.

Titus and his female accomplice opened the trunk and emptied it of papers and golf clubs, throwing them onto the pavement. "Get in the f---ing trunk," Steve heard next.

"About two weeks earlier, I had read a story about someone who was robbed and forced into their trunk and then the car was dumped into the river. That's all I could think about, and I wasn't about to get in that trunk," Steve recalls. With a loaded .45 aimed at his head, he told his assailant, "I'm not getting in the trunk. You can shoot me here, but I'm not going to fit, and I'm not getting in. I'm not!" The large female attempted herself to climb in and couldn't. "He ain't fitting in the trunk," she said to her gun-wielding boyfriend. "Honestly, Mark I thought I was going to be shot in the head right then and there," Steve said later.

"F--- it, get in the back seat," Titus ordered. "Face down!" Crammed inside the tiny, hot back seat of a sports car and in fear for his life, Steve had no idea what lay ahead. "I remember them stopping and buying drugs with my money. They were smoking crack and weed in the car and driving all over the place," Steve said. Titus was driving, and his accomplice was holding Steve with the gun against the back of his head, keeping him face down in the cramped back seat. "Every time, and I mean every time I even lifted my head an inch, I had the gun stuck against my head." Steve remembers slowing down and going over several speed bumps when he thought they were in the local housing projects. At one point the pair of kidnappers pulled up to a location to show off their prey to their drug addicted friends. "Oh, man, check it out. They got a white boy robbed in the back," he remembers hearing one man say, laughing and joking about his predicament. The female got back in the car after what Steve thought was another drug purchase. Titus stepped on the gas and began doing donuts, speeding frantically around the parking lot. "I couldn't have gotten up if I tried. He was driving so crazy. I couldn't believe that making all of this noise and driving a Mustang like a maniac wouldn't attract the cops."

By now, his captors were very high on crack cocaine and marijuana, and driving like Steve McQueen in *Bullit*, only with less control and more speed. Steve knew he had to end this journey. He told his abductors that there was money at the store he owned, and that he would be more than happy to give it to them. Steve told me that he absolutely had to get them to that store. He knew the layout, he knew where the alarms were and more important, he knew where his gun was, a full-size and fully loaded Beretta 92 FS 9mm. A U.S. Navy veteran and military-trained marksman, Steve knew he had one option at this point. He had to get them on familiar territory and end this. "All I wanted to do was go home," he told me.

Titus and his accomplice agreed with Steve's plan to go to the store for more money. Too high to think about the possible consequences to their own lives, they put Steve back behind the wheel of his father's Mustang. "As soon as I pulled out of wherever it was we were, I saw a cop pull up behind us," Steve told me. "Be cool, be cool," said his captors. "Just drive."

"I remember thinking, this can't look right. Certainly this cop has to know something isn't right with this picture," Steve said. "No sooner than I thought that, the police cruiser lit me up. Fortunately, my dad had forgotten to register the expired temporary tags and I was being pulled over."

Not sure exactly what to do, and afraid of being killed, Steve slammed on the brakes and flew out of the driver's door with the vehicle still moving. The police officer jumped from his vehicle and pulled out his gun. "I've been carjacked and robbed!" Steve yelled as loud as he could, throwing his hands in the air. "They robbed me and carjacked me," he screamed as Titus jumped into the driver's seat and took off with the car. Ironically, Steve was "safe," but now found himself staring down the muzzle of a Wilmington police officer's duty gun. With hands in the air, Steve watched as the officer jumped back in his unit and gave chase to the Mustang.

Silence. There was nothing but silence. He found himself alone on the side of a lonely road in an empty parking lot at near 11:30 PM, four and one half hours after his surreal kidnapping had begun. He waited … and waited. "I was there for about 15 or 20 minutes when another cruiser pulls up and this cop asks me to get in the car. It turns out that in Wilmington, they have this really smart law that cops have to stop at red lights when chasing criminals. They wrecked my dad's car into a house and got away because the officer had to give up the chase. Unreal," Steve reported with frustration, "unreal. I had heard the girl say 'Titus, come on.' So I knew his name. I mean how many people can be named Titus? The cops took me all over some of the neighborhoods they thought I had been taken to, and brought guys over for me to look at, but we couldn't find him."

Unable to find his assailants with the officers, Steve was taken to the local police station where he went through mug photos of some of the area's most upstanding citizens. He pointed out a couple of pictures that he was sure were Titus, and then he phoned friends to request a ride home. "I got a call about two weeks later that they had him picked up and charged," Steve said. "I had the opportunity to meet him, but didn't really care to."

Titus was arrested approximately two weeks after shoving a gun in Steve Murphy's face and never did give up the name of his female accomplice. Steve was given the opportunity to meet his assailant at sentencing but chose not to. "All I wanted to do was go on with my life," he told me, "I really didn't care to see his face again." Titus Singleton was charged with numerous crimes, and in January of 2002 he began serving a ten-year jail term after reaching a plea agreement with local prosecutors. His expected release date is fast approaching as this book goes to press.

Talking with Steve about this event was fascinating for a number of reasons. You see, Steve Murphy is a first cousin of mine and also a close friend. He and I spent much time together as we were growing up. I was shocked to find out what happened to him and very happy that he was physically unharmed during the assault and kidnapping against him. One of the first things I asked him was what would have happened if he'd had his gun on him that late afternoon in July. "Mark, as you know, and as I was taught in the military, even if I had been armed when the gun was initially stuck in my face, it is impossible to outdraw a drawn gun. However, I could have ended the ordeal with my own weapon several times afterwards had I had it on me, and the worst would have been that my parents would have had to reupholster the car."

Steve will tell you that now he is much more aware of his surroundings and vows never to get caught off-guard again. He and his family have since relocated from Wilmington, North Carolina. He never leaves home without his gun.

Chapter 6 - The Unarmed Alternatives

Kathy Jackson

"Mark, as you know, and as I was taught in the military, even if I had been armed when the gun was initially stuck in my face, it is impossible to outdraw a drawn gun. However, I could have ended the ordeal with my own weapon several times afterwards had I had it on me and the worst would have been that my parents would have had to reupholster the car."

Though he probably did not feel so immediately after the events related in this chapter, Steve Murphy is an incredibly fortunate individual. It's generally true that you can't outdraw a drawn gun.[1] But the FBI Uniform Crime Reports tell us that the majority of the time when a victim goes with the criminal to a different location, that victim is killed. This means that when an attacker tries to force the victim into a vehicle, it is time for the victim to fight back – right then, right there, using whatever tools the victim has at his or her disposal. If the victim instead chooses to go with the criminal to another location, the odds of survival plummet sharply.

1-For more on this topic, see the work of Dr. Bill Lewinski and others at the Force Science Institute, 124 East Walnut Street Suite 120, Mankato, MN 56001. (507) 387-1290. www.forcescience.org

The lesson Steve Murphy gained from his encounter is a crucial one: today, he's always armed. But even those who are "always armed" might occasionally venture into areas where firearms are forbidden, or where it is functionally impossible to conceal one. What then?

Tool users

Because human beings are tool users, when we think of self-defense we often think first about the tools we would use in self-defense – the hardware.

Hardware is the defensive tools you own: your gun, your knife, your pepper spray, your flashlight, your Kubotan or Persuader. Hardware can also be common items within reach that could be improvised into defensive weapons: your heavy purse, a ball point pen, a screwdriver, a cup of hot coffee. There is literally no end to the number of objects that could be used as weapons, in a pinch. All of them could be defensive hardware.

Of course, hardware doesn't do a lot of good without software to run it. Software is the running system, the "brains" of the hardware. Hardware cannot do anything at all without software telling it what to do. Without software, the best hardware in the world won't accomplish a thing.

In defensive terms, software is the knowledge you've put into your own head, the skills you have forced your muscles to acquire, and the physical reflexes you've deliberately built up over time.

For instance, when the gun is your hardware, your software could be the whole subset of skills that enable you to use a firearm effectively in self-defense. This would include more than simply yanking the trigger. It would include shooting *accurately* and *quickly*. It would also include manipulating the gun with confidence, smooth malfunction clearing, consistent muzzle awareness, and efficient loading and unloading. It would include knowing how to get good hits in poor light, or while running to cover, or with one arm injured, or while holding a child with one hand. And it would definitely include a realistic understanding both of your own limitations when using the firearm and of the laws governing lethal self-defense in your jurisdiction.

For those who plan to defend themselves if they are attacked while unarmed, software would include knowing the effective strike points on a human body so that you don't just flail away ineffectually at an assailant's torso without having any real effect. It could include knowing how to fall without getting hurt and how to strike without breaking your fingers or damaging your wrist joints. Software for unarmed defense could include an accurate mental and emotional understanding of your own physical capabilities so that you make realistic decisions under stress. And it most certainly would include knowing how to cope with an armed assailant when you are not yourself armed with a comparable weapon.

Software upgrades are always available, but lots of people get lazy and just don't bother with them. These folks figure they can putter along just fine as they have been doing. But just like a computer user has to keep her virus protection database updated, it's a good idea for those who are interested in self-defense to make sure their defensive software is always current and not vulnerable to attack simply because it is out of date and working poorly.

For this and many other reasons, it's almost impossible to overstress the importance of quality training, regularly repeated.

Fighting while unarmed

After acquiring a firearm, many gun owners become complacent about unarmed skills. "Why should I learn how to defend myself bare-handed?" they reason. "That's what my gun is for!" Here are several possibilities.

- *Family matters*: You are attacked by someone against whom you must defend yourself, but whom you would rather not shoot.

- *The law sucks:* You left your firearm behind in order to enter an area where firearms are prohibited by law.

- *Access denied:* You are unable to draw your gun for physical or logistic reasons (perhaps the assailant jammed your gun side up against a wall before you could draw, or you became entangled in your seat belt, or your toddler grandson is perched on your hip directly above your firearm).

- *Murphy's Law:* You successfully drew, but your firearm jammed. Now the assailant is right on top of you and you still need to defend yourself.

- *Home sweet home:* You removed your firearm along with your dress pants when you got home, and never wear a holster with your skivvies.

- *Failure of awareness:* Your attacker grabbed your gun out of its holster before you even knew he was there. Now he is armed and you are unarmed and what are you gonna do about it?

- *A threat, but not a lethal threat:* the assailant is considerably smaller than you and appears to be unarmed. A gun isn't appropriate, but he has grabbed you and you need to get away from him. How?

Firearms disarm & retention skills

To my way of thinking, one of the most critical skills that any adult should acquire is the ability to escape from common grabs – and along with it, the knowledge of how to lever a gun out of an assailant's hand. Surprisingly, these techniques do not require a great deal of strength, and they don't even really rely on speed. They only require that the practitioner understands the principles that are in play, and fully commits to using the techniques when appropriate.

As an example of the latter point, I once taught my 5-year-old son how to twist out of a two-handed grab from an adult. With both my hands on his wrist, I could not hold him. When my husband tried to grab his wrist, our son triumphantly slipped away and laughed with glee. Impossible? We weren't really trying? But we were. Each of us tried holding onto his wrist with our full adult strength. He'd simply learned the secret of how to escape from a basic wrist grab.

The principle in play was a simple one, but it has a myriad of applications. It can, perhaps, be expressed most clearly thus: the attacker's body may be stronger than your body. His wrist may be stronger than your wrist. But his wrist is not stronger than your entire body.

All effective handgun disarms are based upon similar principles of leverage and redirection. Some styles add additional power with strikes and blows, although these are not strictly necessary for a well-executed disarm performed at the crucial moment – and the presence of the strike or blow may prevent the beginner from learning the all-important, strength-free principle which forms the foundation upon which the technique is based.

"I will not teach any disarm that doesn't meet the Bambi versus Godzilla test," says well-known firearms instructor Massad Ayoob of the Lethal Force Institute. "By that I mean that the smallest and weakest person in the class must be able to use the technique to take on the most powerful assailant and prevail. Anything less is not acceptable."[2]

Ayoob teaches his students techniques based upon the Lindell system of retentions and disarms, a system which has been taught for many years in American law enforcement. These techniques – which Ayoob teaches in his LFI-2 and subsequent classes – are based upon the work of Jim Lindell, who taught defensive tactics at the Kansas City Regional Police Academy for many years, beginning in the early 1970s. Around that time, there were several well-publicized incidents nationwide in which officers were disarmed and shot with their own weapons. Lindell, an accomplished martial artist, began looking for techniques he could teach his officers which would enable them to protect themselves from disarm attempts. He also taught them how to retrieve the firearm if it had already been snatched.

Though first taught to law enforcement officers, ordinary citizens definitely benefit from learning these techniques. How many school shootings could have been prevented or at least minimized if the adults on the scene had known how to safely snatch a firearm from a child's hand? We'll never know. But having acquired these techniques myself, I'm very strongly of the opinion that every American schoolteacher should under-

2-Author's personal notes from LFI-2 class given summer 2005 at the Firearms Academy of Seattle.

stand the basic disarming principles and have some practice applying them. It could save lives.

Closely related to disarm skills are those required for firearms retention. One question commonly asked is why should anyone learn how to retain a handgun or rifle? After all, if someone is trying to grab your gun the simplest thing to do is to shoot them right off the end of it. But what if the person grabbing isn't someone you want to shoot? It could be a young and foolish family member, for example, or a drunk friend trying to show off. You wouldn't want to shoot such a person, but you would not want to simply hand them a loaded gun, either.

Even if the grabber is clearly a bad guy, it might not be a good idea to shoot immediately. In some circumstances, firing a shot may hit a loved one or other innocent who is standing behind the assailant. You might need to keep the assailant at bay for a brief moment, holding your fire until the backstop is clear.

Guns occasionally jam or fail to fire. While the gun may temporarily be jammed, it probably isn't a good idea to simply hand it to an assailant even so. If Plan A was shooting him, Plan B might be simply keeping the gun away from him, disabling him, and then clearing the jam so that if he gets back up you will be ready to defend yourself.

Finally, the principles involved in gun retentions and disarms are easily applicable to other situations besides a simple gun grab. As my young son learned, these skills can be used to escape from a simple grab. During my first LFI-2 class, to the great amusement of everyone in earshot, Ayoob related the story of how his young daughter defended herself against being "pants-ed" by a school bully using one of these techniques.

Traditional martial arts

Every person who has ever donned a *gi* probably believes that his or her preferred martial art is the Best! One! Ever! Oddly enough, most of these guys are right, because what it takes for most martial arts to succeed is a combination of enthusiasm and dedicated practice. It isn't quite true that any art will do if *you* will do, but it's not far from the truth, either.

There are two basic types of traditional martial arts: "soft" styles, and "hard" styles. A soft-styled art places the emphasis on principles such as balance, leverage, and redirection of the opponent's energy. Hard-styled arts place the emphasis instead on kicks, strikes, and devastating blows.

It is my personal opinion that smaller people looking for a traditional martial art should generally opt to train in a soft-style art rather than in a hard-style art, because the soft arts make more use of the smaller person's lower center of gravity, playing to the element of surprise and using the larger opponent's energy against him. Hard styles, in contrast, are better left to larger people, for whom the hard styles are tailor-made because larger people can naturally put more weight and thus more energy behind strikes and blows.

The biggest weakness of traditional martial arts is that they are *traditional* – that is, full of tradition. In the past, it was common for each master instructor to keep back a few important secrets. As an old man,[3] the master might choose one or two favored students to whom he would pass along *all* the knowledge and skill he had learned over the years, including these key

---

3-No sense using inclusive language here, as it would not be historically accurate. The master instructor was always a man, as were the students. As a result, despite the physical differences between the sexes, very few traditional martial arts feature techniques designed to take advantage of a woman's unique strengths in a mixed contest.

secrets. The favored student never wrote this knowledge down, but committed it to memory and then when he became a master instructor himself, he would in turn pass his knowledge along to his own one or two favored students. This inherently-precarious process eventually caused huge, gaping chunks of important knowledge to fall out of general understanding in many if not most traditional arts. Later instructors, missing that final and essential chunk of understanding, often taught the physical basic movements without fully understanding how or when or why a given technique was designed to work.

Even today, in many traditional martial arts, a great deal of effective self-defense technique is reserved to those who are studying the upper levels of the art. It may take years for a beginner to advance to a level where these effective techniques are taught.

All martial arts schools have a focus, and fall into one of three categories: the exercise model, the sports model, or the self-defense model. Very few traditional martial arts schools actually practice a self-defense model. Most are focused upon either sport or exercise.[4]

Modern martial arts

Modern martial arts include boxing, kickboxing, Jeet Kun Do, Bo Fung Do,[5] PDR,[6] Brazilian jujitsu, Krav Maga and "mixed martial arts."

Although the sharp divide between soft and hard styles is nowhere near as evident in modern martial arts as it is in tradi-

---

4-For a more detailed exploration of this topic, see Marc MacYoung's excellent website, www.NoNonsenseSelfDefense.com
5-System taught by Phil Messina at Modern Warrior, 711 N. Wellwood Ave., Lindenhurst, NY 11757. (888) 692-7746. www.modernwarrior.com
6-Personal Defense Readiness, the system taught by Tony Blauer, Blauer Tactical Systems USA, LLC. 476 Viking Drive #101, Virginia Beach, VA 23452. (877) 773-2748. www.tonyblauer.com

tional ones, the distinction does remain. Typically it shows itself in whether the art emphasizes grappling or whether it emphasizes destructive activity. Again, choose a style that caters to the unique strengths of your own body type.

Many modern arts are billed as "reality based" or "scenario based." That generally means the student will be getting a healthy dose of *context* along with *technique*, an important element that is too often overlooked in the older and more traditional styles. Another thing that many of these systems have in common is that they steal freely from all other systems.[7] That's both their strength – *and* their weakness. What they gain in flexibility and richness of technique, they often lose in cohesiveness and understandable governing principles.

Whether it is a traditional style or a modern one, a top of the line self-defense martial arts school will place a heavy emphasis on improvised weapons – not nunchuks or other "martial arts weapons," but everyday items you might find in your home or yard.

Strategies for the unarmed

When you are otherwise unarmed and your assailant has the upper hand, you must make particular use of the most important weapon you *do* have: your mind.

If you are attacked, react immediately if possible, because your absolute best chance of overcoming the attacker and winning your escape happens immediately. Don't even take time to take a deep breath – respond with sudden, explosive power. Don't hesitate. Make your decision *now* that if you are ever attacked, you will resist with every fiber of your being and that

---

7-And then sue or counter-sue over the use of the material or technique. Ah, modern life!

you will do so instantaneously. Decide now that if you are attacked, you will resist the temptation to throw yourself on the mercy of the merciless. Decide now that you will never grow a wishbone where your backbone ought to be.

If you are unable to react immediately, be aware that temporary compliance *does not* equal total surrender. Maintain constant awareness of the situation and continue looking for your opportunity to escape. Always remember that the goal is ESCAPE – not conquest, not revenge, not justice. Just escape.

Waiting for an opening while temporarily cooperating with the attacker might be the best survival strategy in many situations, but there are a few very specific situations where waiting and cooperating are the worst things the victim can possibly do. A woman forced into a car by an attacker, for example, has an incredibly high chance of getting killed if she complies. Even if it seems highly likely the attacker will kill her right there if she doesn't get in the car, the fact is that right at that moment, the odds are the very best they will ever be for her. They might be lousy odds, but they aren't going to get any better. Similarly, a man forced into a back room on his knees, with his back to the attacker, has just been put into the execution position. Most of the time, when someone is forced into this position, what comes next is a bullet in the back of the skull. Once you are on your knees, you don't have any more choices left, even if you suddenly realize what is about to happen. If you're going to save your own life in such a situation, you have to make the choice to fight back before you're on your knees.

If the attacker is only a robber, he doesn't need to move you away from the location of your first encounter. But rapists and sadistic killers do need privacy or seclusion to finish what they came for. If the bad guy wants to move you to a different location, it's because he will be able to do something to you there that he is unwilling or unable to do to you right where you are. Therefore no matter how bad the tactical situation seems right where you are, it is still the absolute best chance to fight back you will ever have. The odds might be poor and the options lousy, but lousy options now are better than no options later.

Remember that getting to Crime Scene #2 doesn't have to involve moving you many miles – it might be a simple matter of shoving you into a back alley, or getting you to step behind some bushes. Do not allow the criminal to move you even a few feet. Resist any attempt to change your location.

Never, never give up. The sudden violence of a determined attack often leaves victims bewildered, overcome, feeling helpless and disconnected from reality. Fight that feeling! Even if you are temporarily weakened, even if injured, keep looking for opportunities to escape.

Weapons of opportunity

When you must fight bare-handed, be alert to the possibilities in your immediate environment. One way to build this awareness into your mindset is to periodically look around and name all the potential weapons within eyesight. Here are some basic categories to get your creative juices flowing:

- *Bludgeons and clubs.* These are heavy things you can bop the assailant over the head with – or crash into the back of his neck or the side of his knee. A chair would do the trick. So would a baseball bat, a tire iron, a walking stick, a frying pan, or a broom. How about a dinner plate full of spaghetti?
- *Swinging weapons such as chains and coshes.* Try the

home telephone on the end of its cord, a sock full of something heavy, a bike chain.

• *Poking and stabbing implements.* Do you know the second most common stabbing weapon used in aggravated murders in the United States? It's a screwdriver. A pen or a pencil could do the same thing, as could any piece of silverware in the house.

• *Slashing and ripping tools.* Consider the possibilities in a hairbrush or a comb, long fingernails, or the jagged end of a key. Go for the eyes or throat.

• *Distracting items.* A handful of anything small – keys or coins, sand or dirt – can be useful for *brief* distraction, especially when thrown unexpectedly into the assailant's eyes. A cup of hot coffee or even cold water provides a similar distraction. Don't expect the effect to last long. Grab the next thing and keep going.

• *Tools to create distance.* A garden rake, a snow shovel, a broom and a walking stick all have two things in common. First, all could be used as clubs. Second, all could be used to keep an opponent at greater than arm's distance – especially important if the assailant is armed with a knife.

Perhaps none of the above objects strikes you as an ideal weapon. That's true; they're not. But any one of them might be used to buy you time to grab the next weapon, or to open your opportunity to get away.

Along these same lines, if you are ever attacked in your own home by a bare-handed assailant, stay out of the kitchen. There are far too many weapons of opportunity in the average kitchen, and you do not want to lead your unarmed assailant into such a rich arsenal.

Intermediate tools: pepper spray (OC)

Because pepper spray is often legal where firearms are not,[8] it's often suggested as an alternative to private citizen firearms use. Unfortunately, although it can be effective, it's nowhere near the magic talisman that its proponents suggest. Many determined opponents can ignore or fight through their physical responses to its use, and a certain number of people are entirely immune to its effects.

Pepper spray has been on the market since the early 1990s, and is currently in use by thousands of police departments across the United States. Except in very rare circumstances, it is non-lethal. A few folks have no reaction to the stuff at all. But the majority of people do react to it in strong and predictable ways.

Created from extracts of cayenne pepper and properly called Oleoresin Capsicum, or OC, pepper spray's effectiveness is measured in Scoville Heat Units (SHU). It comes in different sizes and different concentrations. Sizes range from tiny enough to hang on your keychain (.5 oz) up to big enough to stop a bear (9 ounces or more) ... *if* the bear is feeling cooperative.

Concentrations of OC, the active ingredient in pepper spray, range from 5 percent up to around 20 percent or even more. While a higher concentration is generally better, the concentration isn't the only consideration. You also want the "hottest" hot you can get, which would be the highest SHU number possible. Most OC products will be marked with both numbers, the SHU and the percentage of OC contained within the inert carrier. Steer clear of products which are not marked with both

---

8-Pepper spray is not legal everywhere. If you are not certain that pepper spray is legal in your jurisdiction, and a basic web search does not turn up the information, call your local police station and ask.

these numbers, because the chances are that the number they're not giving you is unacceptably low.

Here's where it gets complicated: neither the SHU nor the concentration percentage tells the whole story by itself, so you'll need to find a way to take both numbers into account while shopping. For example, say you have a can of 15 percent OC with a claimed SHU of 1,000,000, and you want to compare it with a can of 10 percent OC with an SHU of 2,000,000. There really isn't a common denominator between these two cans, so which one would be more effective in use? To determine that, you can multiply the concentration (15 percent or .15) by the claimed SHU (1,000,000). This gives you a common denominator which allows you to directly compare any two sprays for which you have both numbers.

percent of OC x SHU = effectiveness rating

Physical effects of OC

Among those who do react to pepper spray use, the following responses are the most common, to a greater or lesser degree. Remember, not everyone will react and of those who do react, not everyone will react strongly.

- *Eyes* – The target's eyes water profusely and then slam shut. The effect is somewhat similar to the reaction some people experience while slicing raw onions, but much, much, much stronger. It is physiologically impossible for the target to open his eyes again as long as the OC residue is still in his eyes or on the skin near his eyes. *This temporary blinding is the primary useful effect you need to achieve.*

- *Nose* – Snot production kicks into high gear. Someone who has just been sprayed with OC will often have great masses of snot flowing out of their nose and down the front of their shirt. Icky! Some of the mucus will drip down the back of the nasal passages, producing a claustrophobic drowning sensation.

• *Breathing Passages* – As the product moves into the target's system, all mucous membranes may be affected. The back of the throat and the lungs may feel as if they're burning, and many people begin to feel as if they cannot get a good breath, or as if they are suffocating in their own snot.

• *Skin* – Wherever the OC hits the skin, there will be a burning sensation, which most people report ranges in intensity from mild ("like a really bad sunburn") up through fairly severe ("like a pot of boiling tea just got spilled on me"). The skin turns a blotchy, mottled red and looks inflamed.

• *Other* – Frequently, as a result of the temporary blindness and mucus production, the target will feel claustrophobic. His hands will often go to his face, dropping whatever he was holding, and he may even fall to his knees and curl up into a fetal position.

After you spray the assailant, there will be a brief gap while the spray takes effect. During that 3 to 5 seconds, a lot can happen. Be prepared for this gap and have a plan. Never expect the spray to do all your work for you; be prepared to fight your way to safety if you must.

Even though people resistant to OC are rare, they do exist. If you're going to use OC for defense, you should have an immediate plan for what you will do if the OC does not have any effect at all on your assailant. The most important thing to remember is never, ever quit until your attacker does.

OC in use

Pepper spray traditionally comes in an aerosol can, though there are newer products on the market that deliver the OC charge in other ways. After experimenting with different delivery systems, my recommendation is to stick with a wide spray (cone pattern) aerosol system. This provides a reasonably-distant delivery, a pattern wide enough that precise aim doesn't matter, and the ability to "walk" the spray onto the attacker's face. The newer propulsion systems are often difficult to aim, and provide no ability to adjust to the target's rapid movement. Whichever delivery device you choose, it's a good idea to purchase an inert practice canister along with it so you will know for yourself exactly how your product works. You need to see for yourself what distances are best, how you can expect the wind to affect the product, and how to efficiently deploy it.

No matter which type of product you choose, there is a significant chance that you will receive a dose of OC along with the assailant. *Expect this and plan for it!* Remember that different people experience OC differently, so unless you have been exposed to OC before, you really do not know how your own body will react to it. For this reason, consider taking a class which will allow you to experience OC exposure for yourself. In a good class you will also learn techniques which may allow you to fight through the effects if you are ever sprayed, either inadvertently or by an attacker. If you are unwilling to experience being sprayed in a controlled setting beforehand, and thus do not know how you personally respond to the stuff, I very, very, very strongly recommend that you *do not* carry OC.

A major reason that OC spray works for defense is that – unlike nearly any other intermediate weapon – the defender does not have to physically touch the attacker or get within the attacker's grabbing distance. Staying out of arm's reach is a *major* goal for someone who just wants to get away from an attacker and go home safe!

There's another important reason to make staying out of reach one of your primary goals: cross-contamination. Your best bet for avoiding cross-contamination while escaping the situation is to *spray, dodge, and flee*. Spray the attacker, dodging sharply to one side as you do so, then immediately flee the area. Get outside your attacker's "lunge zone" as quickly as humanly possible. Then keep going. If possible, don't simply run *from* danger, but run *toward* safety, fleeing with a goal in mind.

As you plan your escape strategy, remember that pepper spray's effectiveness depends upon the temporary blinding reaction it creates. The spray will not prevent the attacker from physically grabbing you, especially if you do not step off his line of attack. Even a temporarily blinded attacker may administer a severe or fatal beating once he knows where you are. He may simply lunge straight forward with arms outstretched, hoping to grab you before you escape. Avoid getting bear-hugged by an enraged, blinded assailant by dodging sharply to the side as you spray. Then flee as quickly as you can, escaping in an unexpected direction or at an unexpected angle so your assailant cannot simply lunge for you again.

If the attacker does get his hands on you, plan to *fight* your way to safety, using the OC to briefly distract him as you fight your way free. Do not expect the spray to do all the work for you. And do remember that the empty canister may be an effective bludgeoning weapon.

Intermediate tools: TASER units

First the basics: Taser[9] is a brand name for a type of electronic control device which uses electrical impulses to cause stimulation of the sensory and motor nerves. Unlike the ineffective and gimmicky "stun guns" of an earlier era, Tasers use advanced technology to very effectively eliminate the subject's ability to control his own muscles. At the time of this writing, we are aware of no other device on the market with the stellar reputation that Taser has developed for itself in police use, and certainly no similar product has yet attained the effectiveness of Taser's offerings for private citizens.[10]

At the time of this writing, the C2 is the primary product offered by Taser International for ordinary citizen use.[11] It is different in shape than the typical police units, but uses the same basic technology. One significant difference is that when the police unit is deployed, the power continues for 5 seconds. In contrast, the C2 pulses for 30 seconds, in a varying pattern.

The C2 fires two dart-like metal probes. The probes are each attached to a long, thin piece of insulated wire. As the probes fly, the unit also ejects a large number of tiny little paper scraps with printed serial numbers, to mark the scene for later investigators. The maximum distance at which the C2 can be used is just shy of 15 feet. That's fairly generous for typical defensive situations.

9-TASER® trademark property of TASER International, Inc, 17800 N. 85th St., Scottsdale, AZ 85255-6311. (800) 978-2737. www.TASER.com

10-As with chemical defenses, electric defense devices such as TASER brand products are not legal everywhere. If you are unsure about its legality in your jurisdiction, and a basic web search does not turn up the information, your next best bet is to call TASER International at (800) 978-2737. They'll know the current legal status.

11-The other consumer product currently offered by TASER International, the X26C, is vaguely firearm-shaped and surprisingly bulky. It features a 10-second charge and was first introduced in 2004.

As the probes are fired, the device begins sending an electrical pulse which is intended to travel between the two probes after they hit the target's body. When both probes hit the body, the muscles in the area between the probes will be completely locked up and unable to move because the nerve signals are blocked by "static." This part of the device's function is not based upon pain compliance, but upon disruption of both sensory and motor nerve signals. It cannot be overcome by someone drunk or on drugs or just enraged, because the nerve signals just won't get through.

As the subject is struck by the probes and the circuit is completed, the subject's muscles will usually lock up in involuntary contractions, and he will usually fall to the ground without even the ability to raise his hand to protect his face as he falls. The effect is very striking, and very impressive.

After the initial 30 seconds has expired, the unit can be re-activated indefinitely until the battery dies. The company's literature claims that the unit's battery will last through 50 or more activations; however, my personal observation of a single unit showed a significant drop-off in power at around 10 re-activations. In either case, this should be enough power to solve the problem at hand (and if it's not, there's a mindset problem, not a gear problem).

The C2 in use

If only one probe strikes the assailant, the circuit will not be completed. The target will feel no shock, and experience no incapacitation or restriction of movement. He will, however, feel the dart-like probe striking his body, and is unlikely to be pleased by it.

If both probes land too close together, the circuit completes, but since the area between the probes is so small, the area of true nerve disruption will be similarly limited. In this case, the device basically becomes a pain compliance tool rather than a nerve-disruption device. Having experienced this, I can say that the pain the unit produces when the probes land only inches apart is frankly not that bad. Free movement is typically not restricted, or not significantly restricted, under these conditions.

The ideal strike would place one probe in the upper right quadrant of the torso and the other in the lower left quadrant (or vice versa), running the circuit through the subject's entire body core for maximum effectiveness. As used in real life, the further away from the assailant you are at the moment you fire, the further apart the probes will land – and the greater the likelihood that one of the probes will miss. Conversely, the closer you are, the more likely it becomes that both probes land on target – and the more likely it also becomes that the probes will land too close together for maximum effectiveness.

Cartridges are expensive. At the time of this writing, refills cost around $25 apiece (sold in a two-pack). At this cost, it would be an unusual person who practices even once, let alone practices enough to find marksmanship instinctive under extreme stress. For this reason, I strongly recommend that those who purchase a C2 Taser purchase the laser-equipped variant. Whether you opt for the laser variant or not, it's still crucial that you fire at least a few test cartridges to understand how your unit works.

The C2 also features something called "drive stun capability." That means that if one or both of the probes miss the assailant's body, you can instead drive the device straight into his body while the current is flowing, and it'll light him up just as the older stun guns did. Unfortunately, when the drive stun is used by itself, it's only slightly painful, not excruciating. It is certainly *not* significant enough to stop an angry or inebriated assailant. All he has to do is reflexively jerk his hand or body away from the unit at first contact, and from that point it is absolutely easy for anyone with any degree of fighting experience to solve the rest of the problem without getting shocked again.

When only one probe is in the assailant's body, you can use the drive stun as far away from that probe as possible and that will lock him up. But remember that if he knocks your hand away (which he may still be able to do), or when the battery dies (which it eventually will), the current is gone instantly and you will be within close contact distance of an enraged, fully adrenalized criminal who is no longer incapacitated. Better have a plan to deal with that.

If both probes hit the ideal distance apart and the assailant is immediately and completely disabled by the current, the next step is to drop the device to the ground and run to safety. According to company literature, Taser International will reimburse you for the cost of the unit, or replace it, when you use this strategy. That part is wonderful. But now the downside: How far can you run in 30 seconds or less? Is it further than an enraged, fully-adrenalized assailant can follow? Remember, one of the reasons police love their Tasers is because after the ride is over, it's over – there are no aftereffects for the person upon it is used. Once the current shuts off, the subject is completely unimpaired, with no residual weakness or other problems to worry about. So when the current of your C2 shuts off, your assailant is just as fast and as powerful as he was before, he's going to be enraged because the Taser ride didn't feel too good, and you've just left the unit behind so he knows you are now unarmed. Better hope you're within 30 seconds of safety, or have a solid back up plan for what to do if you're not.

The wires to which the probes are attached are surprisingly fragile. Anyone who's been tased before knows this and probably has a plan to do something about it. Keep in mind that most violent assailants are recidivists and have been arrested before, and the Taser is a common tool in police use.

Used as police use the tool – typically deployed at a distance, or from behind if possible, with a lethal-force backup, and employed primarily as a compliance device rather than as a self-defense device – the Taser is a wonderful tool that can save, and has saved, many lives. When it's used in the types of contexts where ordinary people would use it, it is a good tool but there are still some significant limitations associated with its use. This is particularly true for those who are not trained in martial arts, and for those who do not have the mindset to do whatever it takes to debilitate someone enough to prevent them from continuing the attack after the current shuts off if the attack does not occur within 30 seconds of a safe haven.

Knives

Knives are, of course, lethal weapons with all that entails. Among other things, this means that pulling a knife on an assailant is the legal equivalent of firing a gun at him, or using any other form of lethal force against him. Legally speaking, there is no difference at all between using a gun or using a knife. They are both deadly weapons which may legally be used only when there is an immediate and otherwise unavoidable danger of death or grave bodily harm to the innocent.

Nevertheless, there may be a place for a defensive knife in the firearm owner's pocket. There are a few municipalities where guns are outlawed, but knives are legal. Although it is generally very much preferable to keep your distance and not get close unless you cannot avoid it, there are a few circumstances where personal defense with a knife might even be preferable to defense with a gun – such as in a very crowded area with many innocent bystanders.

Knives require a great deal of trained skill to use well, however. And they require a very *personal* commitment to doing violence against the attacker. They are not a tool for the non-athletic, the squeamish or the faint of heart.

Conclusion

Regardless of which alternative weapon you choose to carry, it's important to remember that your "software" – the technical knowledge and physical skillset needed to effectively defend yourself with your chosen tool – is every bit as important as the hardware you choose. Always load good software, and always keep your software up to date!

Chapter 7 - A Savage Gunfight

Mark Walters

Tampa, Florida is a beautiful place. I can attest to that after spending nearly 15 years there as a resident. Like many people who move to Florida, I did so to escape the colder weather of the northern cities that I had been transferred to over the years after graduating from college. Meeting friends was difficult in a new place but not impossible, and like most people, I consider myself lucky if I can count my true lifelong friends on one hand. Vincent Savage is one of them.

Vincent is one of the most interesting people I have ever known. Well traveled around the world, he has spent time working and sightseeing in areas of the globe where most people would never venture, from the Middle East to being a current property owner in Colombia, South America. Shortly after settling down in Tampa, Vincent survived an encounter that he thought would be more likely to happen in some of the third world countries he had visited, rather than on the streets of his newly adopted, sun drenched home town. Like me, he makes friends easily, and one sunny Saturday afternoon, heading over to a buddy's home to spend some time outside would almost end his life.

Vincent was on his way to pick up his friend. He was approximately 30 minutes ahead of schedule, and he knew he was going to have to wait. "I knew I was going to be early," Vincent told me during our interview. "I didn't really care. I just wanted to get outside and have some fun, maybe pick up my friend and hit the range or something."

As he pulled into his friend's driveway, Vincent noticed a car with the trunk lid up, parked in the alley next to the house. "I don't know what made me do it. I guess it just didn't look right so I got out to investigate," he said. Walking towards the car, he heard noises and voices coming from inside a wooden shed on his friend's property. "They were speaking Spanish. I speak Spanish as well, but I couldn't make out exactly what they were saying from where I was so I decided to take a closer look."

Vincent approached the shed, and being well schooled in the ways of the world, he drew his Sig Sauer P226. Holding the weapon down and to the side of his right leg, he approached the shed doors. "I heard them stop what they were doing. I can only guess to this day, but I believe they may have heard me coming. I reached for the latch on the shed, and before I could get to it, the doors swung open like they had been kicked."

POW. POW. POW. "All I could see was muzzle flashes, so I raised my right hand." Standing in front of Vincent were two Cuban immigrants (later found to have come to Florida as part of the 1980 Mariel boat lift). They had just been interrupted by Vincent as they were burglarizing his friend's property. Vincent Savage now found himself in a face to face gunfight with two armed and violent young men.

POW. POW. POW. Vincent instinctively returned fire at bad-breath distance as he moved desperately to his left in an attempt to get cover on the side of the shed. "I knew I was hit right away. I could feel the pain in my right thumb as I pulled the trigger. I remember intentionally trying to shoot the guy directly in his face." As Vincent sheltered behind the false safety of the wooden walls, the duo began firing again. The wood splintered as Vincent ducked the incoming rounds. One shattered the wooden wall, fragmented, and found its way to the right side of Vincent's face. Another round grazed the right side of his stomach.

Vincent fired at the shed as he ran across the yard, fleeing the property in an attempt to get to safety. He bolted across the street and over a fence, and dropped his weapon before finding himself inside a convenience store. Bleeding from his hand, eye, and a grazing wound to the stomach, he asked the owners to call the police. Within minutes, the area was swarming with law enforcement officers, and Vincent was on his way to the hospital.

"I had been hit in the thumb on my gun hand. I guess it's a testament to the fact that people will instinctively fire at the weapon during a confrontation. As I moved to cover on the left side of the shed, and as they fired through the wooden walls, I took a fragment of lead just below my right eye, and another fragmented round to the right side of my stomach," Vincent says today.

Fortunately, none of Vincent's wounds were life-threatening, although his right thumb is now one half inch shorter than his left, leaving him maimed forever. Both men were later caught in the dragnet set up by Tampa police. Vincent had shot one of the criminals directly in the abdomen, seriously wounding him. The second offender was not hit even though the lead was flying at a distance of less than four feet. Both men were prosecuted, found guilty, and did time for the crimes they committed that afternoon. Vincent was found to be acting in self-defense, and no charges were filed against him. Police later recovered his Sig Sauer P226 and it was returned to him after the investigation was completed.

Vincent Savage continues to reside in the greater Tampa area, and spends his time traveling with his wife and children between his home in Tampa and his wife's homeland of Colombia. As one of the first CCW permit holders in Florida after the 1987 landmark Florida law was passed, he has used the incident as motivation to continue his firearm training and self defense instruction. Vincent is now a certified firearms trainer in the United States and Colombia with Suarez International, an internationally recognized Force on Force training school.

Chapter 8 - The Physiology of Danger

Kathy Jackson

Pretty much everyone these days has experienced the frustration of dealing with a computer that has bogged down while downloading a large file which takes up the majority of the computer's resources. If the system is engaged on such a major task and you go to check your email, you will probably notice some delays in accessing the email program and logging in, or in storing, retrieving and displaying downloaded emails. You might even receive error messages caused by a loss of data during the transfer. All of these events are normal, and not a sign that something is wrong with the computer. It's just what happens when the computer nears the limits of its finite resources.

Similarly, during a life-threatening encounter, a large number of the finite resources within your physical body, your emotional capacity, and especially within your information-processing brain will be forced to the utter limit. Some strange but predictable *and completely normal* perceptual changes can result. Except for the physical changes caused by the basic fight-or-flight response, not everyone will experience the perceptual reactions listed in this chapter. Of those who do experience perceptual distortions, not everyone will experience them in the same way or to the same degree. Yet these are all common and normal reactions, and the majority of people will experience one or more of these physiological effects of stress during a life-threatening event.[1]

All of these perceptual changes are closely interrelated, and in many ways they all play into each other. This chapter will give you information you need to know about how your body and brain work together under stress. Once you know what may happen, what types of reactions your body and mind together can create under stress, you will be to a large degree inoculated against fearing these reactions. You'll be able to continue to concentrate on the task at hand, doing the important job of saving your own life, without being unduly frightened or distracted by these unusual but not abnormal sensations.

There is another reason you need to understand these phenomena. That is because you may – no, you will – find yourself needing afterward to explain the actions you took during a lethal force incident. If you drew your gun, you will need to articulate to someone why you drew your gun. If you fired, you'll need to explain why you fired. In the immediate aftermath of the encounter, and in your memory later, you may find that one or more of these phenomena may loom large in your understanding of the traumatic event and how it happened. In your interactions

---

1-The most easily-obtained brief synopsis of various studies giving specific percentages to each perceptual phenomenon may be *Perceptual and Memory Distortions During Officer Involved Shootings* (2008 update), given as a presentation by Dr. Alexis Artwohl, Ph.D. during an AELE seminar in 2008. It is available online at http://www.aele.org/law/2008FPJUN/wb-19.pdf. More in-depth material may be obtained from the original article that the 2008 presentation is based upon, *Perceptual and Memory Distortions During Officer Involved Shootings* (2002), by Dr. Alexis Artwohl, published in the October 2002, Volume 71, Number 10 edition of the FBI Law Enforcement Bulletin, available online at http://www.fbi.gov/publications/leb/2002/oct2002/oct02leb.htm#page_19. The summarized studies show quite a bit of variation in the percentages of individual perceptual distortions, probably due to differences in study design and methodologies; however, studies from various sources consistently show the multiplicity of factors mentioned in this chapter are common phenomena. In all studies the author is aware of, a majority of participants experienced auditory exclusion, tunnel vision, or time distortion effects.

with police immediately after your incident, in your explanation to your defense attorney and your loved ones, and even in your own memory later, your knowledge of these reactions may make a critical difference in how you understand what happened, and in how you communicate the events to others. Some of these phenomena can trip you up, skew your perceptions of time and spatial coordinates, and in other ways distort your understanding. You need to anticipate the tricks your mind may play on you, so that you can accurately report what happened and explain these things to others.

These reactions are a large part of the reason why most firearms instructors and all lawyers tell people not to give police a detailed statement during the immediate aftermath of an event. Your perceptions have been skewed by the incredible stress of a life-threatening event, and you need time to regain some of your perspective.[2]

Body alarm reaction: fight or flight

The perceptual changes people experience under stress actually begin as physical changes, an expression of the body alarm reaction. The body alarm reaction is an instinctual response to stress, and it is common to all mammals. The strongest and most significant expression of the body alarm reaction is commonly called the *fight or flight* response. Dr. Walter Cannon, working out of the Harvard Medical School, first coined the term *fight or flight* back in 1915.[3]   Other phrases you may hear for the same

2-It's important to note here that some of your lost perspective may never be regained. That, too, is a normal reaction to an abnormal event.
3-The term was first used in *Bodily Changes in Pain, Hunger, Fear, and Rage. An Account of Recent Researches into the Function of Emotional Excitement.* New York, D. Appleton, 1915. Cannon also served as president of the American Physiological Association.

collection of physical responses are the *acute stress response* or *hyperarousal*.

During the fight or flight response, the heart and lungs speed up, pumping extra oxygen into the blood stream. The blood pressure skyrockets as blood vessels in the extremities constrict, while the blood vessels responsible for large muscle movement dilate widely to deliver that extra oxygen where it is most needed. Released into the bloodstream, sugar provides fuel for large motor activity.[4] The digestive system abruptly shuts down; you may feel a "churning" in the gut as a result, with or without actual nausea. The pupils dilate, taking in more light. The eyes and mouth go dry as the salivary glands and tear ducts are inhibited. Later you may remember an odd chemical taste in the mouth, related to the hormone release. (Sometimes people call this "the taste of fear.") The bladder and bowels may relax and shed their contents.[5,6]

All of these physical changes immediately follow the release of stress-related hormones. Because it is an endocrine response, the physical changes are nearly instantaneous. Your endocrine system simply releases the stress hormones all at once and off you go – fast and furious. This hormonal release is commonly called an *adrenaline dump*. It's named after the most well-known of the stress hormones, adrenaline, which is also called epinephrine.

4-Diabetics should be especially aware of the role of blood sugar during acute stress. During a highly-stressful event, the blood sugar rises sharply; following the event, blood sugar plummets even more sharply. Perhaps a piece of hard candy should be stored alongside the extra ammunition.
5-*Deadly Force Encounters: What Cops Need to Know to Mentally and Physically Prepare for and Survive a Gunfight*, by Dr. Alexis Artwohl and Loren W. Christensen. Boulder, CO; Paladin Press; 1997, p 38.
6-*On Combat: The Psychology and Physiology of Deadly Conflict in War and in Peace*, by Lt. Col. Dave Grossman with Loren W. Christensen. Warrior Science Publications, 2008, p 8-11.

Epinephrine speeds up your body, and signals the release of norepinephrine. In addition to its other physical effects, norepinephrine is a neurotransmitter. That may be why its release in large quantities into the bloodstream can affect the mind's perceptions so strongly. Norepinephrine in particular is a psychoactive chemical. It has a significant, measurable effect on how, and how fast, your brain is able to process information.

Pain resistance and physical strength

During the body alarm reaction, the body also releases endorphins that are natural painkillers. In medical jargon endorphins are *endogenous opioids*. Endogenous means the body produced the substance naturally, within itself. Want to guess what an opioid is? Here are some examples from the same family of chemicals: opium, morphine, codeine, and heroin.[7] These narcotic drugs mimic the effects of the opioids called endorphins that are naturally produced within the human body under stress. Endorphins are powerful natural painkillers that block pain receptors in the body.[8]

The good news here is that when you are ramped up to deal with an extreme threat to your own survival, you may not feel any pain or even realize you are hurt until long after the event is over. This is one reason people who have been shot will sometimes say, "I did not even feel the shot," or "I did not real-

---

7-An opioid is produced within the body, while an opiate is any of a number of compounds typically purified from opium that target the same receptors and otherwise mimic the behavior of the naturally-produced bodily opioids. The listed drugs are actually opiates, not opioids. But chemically speaking, opioids and opiates are close members of the same family and have similar effects on human physiology.

8-Incidentally, it is just as possible to become addicted to the body's own endorphins as it is to become addicted to artificial drugs. The difference is that many "adrenaline junkies" perform useful roles in society and, in fact, become addicted to the rush of doing battle against fires, bad guys, or national enemies. See Deadly Force Encounters, p 27-28.

ize I had been shot."[9] The body's own natural painkillers can mask even severe pain and allow you to finish the job of saving your own life without being distracted by injury. Sometimes, of course, the physical damage will include a cut nerve or other damage that actually prevents feeling, but many times the failure to feel an injury immediately when it happens is simply part of this naturally produced imperviousness to pain. This means that after an incident, even if you don't think you were hurt, you should *look* at yourself. Visually inspect yourself and your family members. Your eyes may tell you what your nerves temporarily cannot.

This is also a period of superhuman, unbelievable strength. It's caused by the stress hormones being released in the body, the speeding-up of the heart and lungs, the increased blood flow to the large muscles of the body as the body prepares to make a superhuman effort to defend itself by fighting or fleeing. The large muscles of your body get stronger for a time, able to make an incredible effort. You know the stories, the 60 year old grandmother who lifted a car that had rolled onto her grandchild, the man who held up the cracking timbers in the mine and allowed his mining buddies to escape to safety – all of these types of stories simply reflect what the human body can do under the extreme encouragement of the body alarm reaction.

The payoff for this period of incredible speed, strength, and pain resistance is the *relaxation effect* which inevitably follows. After the entire event is over, there will be a precipitous drop in hormone production. As soon as the pressure is off, the same physical reactions which sped you up, increased your strength, and made you nearly impervious to pain will rebound and make

9-*Into the Kill Zone: A Cop's-Eye View of Deadly Force*, by David Klinger. San Francisco, CA; Jossey-Bass; 2004. See p114-115.

you collapse like a marionette puppet with its strings cut. Your knees go weak and you just gotta sit down for a moment. Human beings are a lot like spaghetti noodles – after we've been in hot water, we go a bit limp. Again, that's a normal reaction and does not necessarily mean anything is wrong, but if it happens to you, *do* visually check yourself to be certain you are not bleeding unawares.

Motor skills

Under the influence of epinephrine and related compounds, large motor movements become easy, and can be done faster and with more power than ever before. The trade off for this increased speed and power is that fine motor control will suffer.

You've probably experienced the loss of fine motor skills to a lesser degree when you were nervous during a job interview or some other stressful interaction. You drop your pencil, or you get flustered and can't seem to write as neatly as you want. You're unhappy that you're late for work and you can't get your key into the ignition of your car. Some researchers have even postulated that the loss of fine motor skills is the *inevitable* result of a fast heart rate, and that these skills will *always* decline to the point of uselessness as the heart speeds up under stress. Not so, reports Dr. Bill Lewinski in issue #64 of the Force Science News:

> *The idea that a high heart rate causes a loss of fine motor skills is a myth. The culprit is fear or anger, not heart rate per se.*
> *It's true that if you reach a very high heart rate through physical exertion and are trying to both sight a handgun and breathe, for example, you may experience some MINOR issues with fine psychomotor skills. However, keep in mind that*

well-trained biathlon athletes fire accurate shots with a pulse of 180 bpm, and even mediocre sandlot basketball players under the high pulse rates of a very competitive game make pretty good shots.

We much more noticeably lose psychomotor skills under fear or anger, primarily because of our inability to focus attention properly when distressed. The key is training. With a proper training program that allows you to repeatedly practice your skills while under a high degree of stress, you will build your confidence and reduce the impact of negative emotions so that you can maintain your fine-motor dexterity when faced with real-life challenges. In other words, good training can help you build a history of successful performance under high stress.[10]

When you are frightened or upset, your fine motor skills will certainly decline. But good training – which includes skill development, regular practice, competitive pressure and emotionally meaningful force-on-force exercises – will lessen your fear and improve your ability to control what your hands and fingers are able to do under the severe stress of a lethal encounter. And this is true regardless of what your heart rate may do in reaction to the event.

Tremors – "He was shaking in his boots"

Along with this typical loss of fine motor skills, you may experience tremors, a physical shaking that typically starts in the fingers of your non dominant hand, moving to your domi-

10-Force Science Newsletter #164 accessed online at http://www.forcescience.org/fsinews/2007/01/new-free-on-line-law-journal-for-police-corrections on 8/12/2009. Force Science News is published by the Force Science Institute, 124 East Walnut Street, Suite 120, Mankato, MN 56001. (507) 387-1290. www.forcescience.org

nant hand and then shortly thereafter to your lower extremities, your feet and knees. Rock climbers call it "sewing machine leg" or "Elvis leg" as the lower body and knees begin to shake and vibrate uncontrollably.

Both the loss of fine motor skills and the physical tremors mean that as you look for shooting techniques for self-defense, you need to put a premium on those techniques which do not rely upon fine motor skills. Is shooting itself a fine motor skill? Of course it is! But you can and should minimize your reliance on fine motor skills whenever and wherever possible, if you are intending to save your own life during a highly stressful encounter.[11]

All of these physical reactions, in turn, interact with your mind's ability to perceive what is going on around it, and to put these perceptions into perspective.

Tachypsychia – life at the speed of thought

Everything started to slow down at that point. ... I couldn't seem to make my body move fast enough. He seemed to be moving slowly, too; his gun was coming out slow.[12]

Tachypsychia[13] literally means *the speeding mind*, and it refers to several closely-related time distortion effects. Under extreme stress your mind begins to process information faster than it ever has before. Since exterior time does not speed up to match your body's internal overdrive speed, your brain may

---

11-Some of the premier work in this area has been done by Massad F. Ayoob, as detailed in his book *Stressfire, Vol. 1: Gunfighting for Police: Advanced Tactics and Techniques*. Police Bookshelf, 1986. The shooting techniques Ayoob recommends are designed to take advantage of the body's unique strengths and weaknesses during a high-stress encounter.
12-*Into the Kill Zone*, p 95.
13-Not all researchers use this specific term, but the reactions it describes are common, and commonly studied.

distort the timing of the incoming data, a distortion you perceive as time itself doing unusual things. In reality, the rest of the world continued its normal course of placing a mere 60 seconds in every minute, while your brain kicked into high gear to try to solve the problem.

Typically tachypsychia is experienced as a visual slow-down, where external events look like they're moving in slow motion. You may feel as if you're running through molasses, or as if events are happening quickly but something is making you unable to move at your normal speed. You may even experience a sensation of being "paralyzed" or unable to move.[14] In fact, you are probably moving faster than you ever moved before in your life, but your perception of elapsed time is skewed.

You may instead experience this distortion as a speeding up of external time: "Everything happened so fast! It was all just a blur!" In either case, the important factor is that your internal clock is not in sync with the rest of the world.

Tachypsychia is one reason you must never be specific when the responding officers ask you how long the event took or how quickly you responded. The only truthful answer to such questions is, "I don't know." That's the absolute truth, no matter how firmly you might feel otherwise. You simply do not know whether the tachypsychia effect has skewed your perception of elapsed time. Your mind is not trustworthy to report the timing or the sequence of events that happen under extreme stress.

Tunnel vision and auditory exclusion

I fired five rounds. My vision changed as soon as I started to shoot. It went from seeing the whole picture to just the suspect's

---

14-Although some people do freeze entirely during a high-stress event, this is not common for the trained individual. What is more common is the perception of freezing, which witnesses either never observe at all, or report as a very, very brief interval in a fast-moving situation.

head. Everything else just disappeared.[15]

When in the presence of a deadly threat, human minds focus every bit of the organism's attention on the perceived danger, to the exclusion of everything else around. The eyes still see, the ears still hear, but the brain is screening out everything except that most critical to survival. It's as if the brain just came along and held a pair of binoculars to your eyes, cutting off all perception of your periphery and magnifying the essential event. Your brain is saying, "LOOK AT THAT! *THAT* is what is about to kill us. Look at it!"

In some cases the attention may be focused upon the attacker's entire body, but in other cases the attention becomes fixated on the most significant perceived threat – the muzzle of the gun, the blade of the knife, the moving club. The eyes go to the threat to the exclusion of all other visual inputs. The ears hear nothing, or hear only that which they are tuned to hear. The ears may not hear the sound of gunfire at all, or it may only sound like a soft, "pop" instead of the loud boom ordinarily associated with firing a weapon. There's no audio, no soundtrack, to some events.

I knew the guy was shooting at us because I saw him shooting, but I didn't really hear the rounds going off. The audible start-up and "BANG!" that usually happens when you pull the trigger wasn't there. It was just a soft "pop, pop, pop." He fired nine rounds at us – all misses. My partner fired four, and I fired two. At the time, I didn't know my partner fired because I didn't hear his shots. In fact, when it was over, I asked him, "Did you shoot, or was it just me?"[16]

15-*Into the Kill Zone*, p 99.
16-*Into the Kill Zone*, p 87.

Both tunnel vision and auditory exclusion are among the most common reactions experienced under extreme stress. Both can be incredibly dangerous during a critical encounter. They can also help you survive. The body causes these reactions to focus your attention and help you save your own life, but at the same time, the focusing-in itself can create new hazards.

• You may not hear or see the attacker's friends. Remember: bad guys have friends, too. Not every criminal is a lone wolf. Sometimes wolves come in packs.

• You may not hear or see important auditory or visual cues which the non-involved bystander clearly hears or clearly sees. You may not even see the bystander.[17]

• You may not see the arriving officers. You may not hear the command to stop, to hold your fire.[18]

Because of this, it's important to realize that you will probably need to fight against this human tendency to tunnel in. Be aware of the danger it poses to you. Break out of fixating on the gun or knife; if you need to shoot, deliberately force your attention to the assailant's body, away from his weapon. Immediately after you shoot, physically turn your head and *look* around you. Break out of the tunnel.

By the way, although extreme "tunneling-in" effects are definitely part of the body's reaction to stressful events, to a lesser degree they are also common in daily life as the brain's way of assigning priority status to different tasks. When you've selected one task as being worth your full and undivided attention, you are much less likely to notice other events happening

17-And – quite apart from moral considerations – this is one significant reason never to do anything which you would not be comfortable with a witness observing. Witnesses often exist who were entirely unobserved by participants.
18-Always remember: you do not have a magical halo above your head that identifies you as the good guy to responding officers. All they know when they arrive on scene is that you are a person with a smoking gun standing over a bleeding body.

right in front of you – even something as apparently obvious as a gorilla walking into a confined area, beating its chest, jumping up and down, and walking slowly away.[19] Tunnel vision is indeed a powerful force.

After a deadly force encounter, police investigators, lawyers and prosecutors, and even friends and family are likely to ask the survivor questions such as, "What do you MEAN, you didn't see the other witness? He was standing right there!" or "How could you simply not hear the person who was screaming in your ear ...?" The implication is that the survivor is lying about what he saw, or heard, or remembered. But the surprising truth is that multiple scientific studies show human beings simply cannot absorb and do not process multiple tracks of focus-intensive events. This is true in a calm laboratory setting and it is even more true during stressful, life-or-death events.

Estimating size and distance

When I opened the door and stepped out, there was this fourteen-year-old standing there with this gun pointed at me. Now I never saw him. All I saw was the gun. I had no idea who was holding it. It could have been an eight-foot-tall transvestite or a ninety-year-old lady for all I knew. All I saw was the barrel, the cylinder, the trigger guard, and the trigger. The barrel looked really big. It looked like a cannon.[20]

§ § §

During a violent shoot-out I looked over, drawn to the sudden mayhem, and was puzzled to see beer cans slowly floating

19-*Gorillas in our midst: Sustained inattentional blindness for dynamic events,* by D.J. Simons and C.F. Chabris (1999). Perception, 28, 1059-1074. A copy of this study may be requested online at **https://www.psych.uiuc.edu/reprints/index.php?site_id=1**
20-*Into the Kill Zone,* p 117.

through the air past my face. What was even more puzzling was that they had the word Federal printed on the bottom. They turned out to be the shell casings ejected by the officer who was firing next to me.[21]

Estimating size and distance becomes very difficult under life-threatening stress. In part, this is a direct result of tunnel vision and related effects, an optical illusion caused by focusing sharply on the threat and ignoring its surroundings. This sharp focus eliminates a lot of the external visual input which would otherwise enable you to accurately judge size and distance.

Distortions of size and distance may also be the result of the brain being overwhelmed with data pouring in too fast to store in the normal manner, like an assembly-line worker in one of those old black and white comedy movies where someone turned the conveyor belt speed to "ridiculous." The worker moves faster, then faster and faster again, but at some point things on the belt start slipping past, getting away. Size and distance, being difficult for many to estimate even in calm conditions, often slip past a brain that is overstressed and forced to move at high speed.

Here's the *really* bad news: your mind is the only instrument by which you have to judge both the distance itself and your own perceptual abilities. The inputs your mind normally relies upon have been restricted by the stress reaction, and you simply *cannot know* whether that has affected your perception of distance. Because the mind can be fooled in this way, until there has been an objective investigation of the physical evidence on the scene, the involved individual literally has no way

---

21-*Perceptual and Memory Distortions* (2002).

of knowing whether or not they are among the fortunate ones who did not experience distance and proportional distortions.

This means that the *only* truthful answer when asked to judge the distance at which a violent encounter happened is, "I don't know." You do not know to what extent, if any, tunnel vision and other visual distortions skewed your perception of the distance to the threat. Your brain was functioning with distorted inputs and that means its output is suspect. Don't trust it! Regardless of your feelings about distance and related questions during the event and in the immediate aftermath, you truly do not know how far away the attacker was, how big the weapon was, how long the knife blade was, or any other proportion-related detail.

Precognition

Precognition is a response to subconsciously-perceived stimuli. It can happen during a high-stress event without any ability to articulate what you reacted to. Later, if you analyze it, you will probably be able to figure out what the input or stimuli was, and will probably be able to articulate why you concluded what you concluded. At the time, you just "know" something, without analysis.

Sounds kind of mystic, doesn't it? But it's not mystic at all. While precognition might be called a "sixth sense" or a "hunch," it can easily be explained scientifically – and without resorting to mumbo jumbo either. Here's the explanation: The trained eye sees what the untrained eye does not.

Have you ever been driving down the freeway when you saw a car which did not have its turn signal on but when you saw it, you thought, "That car is going to come over into my lane"

– and a moment later, it did? That's what precognition looks like. You've been driving for years, and your mind has learned to associate certain cues with the events that follow. Your eye sees another driver's car swerve slightly to the left as the driver glances over his shoulder, then the car changes lanes. The subconscious mind sees the glance and the swerve, associates the data, makes a conclusion, and it feeds the conclusion but not the reasoning into your conscious mind. Consciously, you simply *felt* that the driver was about to change lanes. And he did.

Okay, why does this matter to you as an armed individual? Someday, you may need to explain your actions to the authorities. If so, "I just *felt* he was going to attack" will not help your case in the slightest, while "I saw this particular motion or series of motions, and – based upon my training and experience – that led me to conclude an attack was imminent" may be a great help indeed. During the event you may just *feel* or *believe*, acting on those beliefs to save your life. Trust your gut! But after the event, you must be prepared to rationally analyze and justify your own reactions, especially the ones you didn't fully understand at the time.

The *trained* eye sees what the untrained eye does not; the *trained* mind perceives and correlates data the untrained mind may disregard. For this reason (among many others), truly professional firearms instruction and ongoing self-defense training may well become your necessary allies, both during the event and then later in the justice system and within the court of your own conscience.[22]

22-This discussion of precognition was heavily drawn from notes taken during Massad Ayoob's LFI-1 and Judicious Use of Deadly Force Instructor classes. The author strongly recommends LFI-1 in particular for serious defensive students. See also *Physio-psychological Aspects of Violent Encounters,* a video produced by LFI and available through the Police Bookshelf.

Memory distortions

One of the most striking things to come out of the recent renaissance in human memory research is the finding that human memory does not simply record external events as if on an internal human videotape. Rather, memory is a complex and sometimes quirky creative process that is not yet fully understood.[23] Although the common perception is that highly-emotional events *must* be remembered accurately and in full, the truth is that the more emotionally charged the situation, the more likely it is that memory will fail or be incomplete.[24] Again, this is normal and predictable, well understood by memory researchers.[25]

In addition to memories placed out of sequence (or sometimes, familiar actions performed out of sequence), other related distortions include small, trivial things looming large in one's memory, especially in the immediate aftermath of the incident. At the same time, critically important details may be lost. These memories may surface later, or they may be gone forever.

Confabulation

Closely related to other memory distortions is a process called *confabulation*. No, it's not a fancy word that means someone lied! Rather, confabulation is the normal process by which an active brain fills in the information that "must have" happened, given the events the brain knows to have occurred before or after the data gap.

23-*Perceptual and Memory Distortions* (2008), p 19-6.
24-*Critical Incident Amnesia: The Physiological Basis and Implications of Memory Loss During Extreme Survival Stress Situations*, by Lt. Col. Dave Grossman and Bruce K. Siddle. Published in The Firearms Instructor: The Official Journal of the International Association of Law Enforcement Firearms Instructors, Issue 31, Aug 2001. It may be accessed online at Lt. Col. Grossman's website, **http://www.killology.com/article_amnesia.htm**. Essential quote: "Unfortunately, by their very nature, traumatic situations will inevitably result in memory impairment...The greater the stress, the greater the potential will be for these memory problems to occur."
25-Although, unfortunately, *not* by all investigators and prosecuting attorneys.

On a more physical level, confabulation is very similar to the way your brain fills in the missing area around a blind spot. To understand this effect, cover your left eye and focus your right eye intensely on the circle below. Then move the book slowly closer to and then away from your face. At some point, the square will seem to disappear. You have just experienced the famous blind spot, a phenomenon most people are at least vaguely familiar with from school science classes.

The surprising thing about the blind spot isn't that it exists. After all, your optic nerve has to be located somewhere; the blind spot is that area of your eyeball where the nerve itself obscures visual reception. Not all that amazing.

What *is* amazing is that your brain is primed to prevent you from ever noticing your own blind spot. When confronted with missing data, the brain takes its best guess about what should be there, and supplies it for you. And it does this *without your conscious awareness* of what just happened. The missing black square doesn't just become nothingness; it becomes white to match the rest of the page. Without even consulting you, your brain chooses the most likely interpretation of the missing data. If the page were purple and the missing square white, you would perceive that the missing white square became purple to match the surrounding area. Based on the surrounding data, the brain fills in the missing piece with the most likely match.

In a similar way, when the brain is confronted with missing data in the memory stream, it fills in the blanks. *And it often does so without the conscious awareness of the person whose brain it is*.

The thing to note here is that despite our usual perceptions, memory really isn't a continuous stream. It might be somewhat akin to a series of still frames from an old movie film, with some data missing between each and every frame. Normally, this makes little or no difference. But as external events speed up or become more stressful, more data goes unrecorded between frames. When the film is "played" later by the conscious person trying to understand what happened, the missing data is supplied not by conscious thought, but by a natural and mostly unconscious process of filling in the blanks.

As a result of this, if you've been in a life-threatening encounter, no matter how desperately you wish to know what "really happened," and no matter how hard others push you to tell every last detail, it's important *not* to force memories into being, and *not* to speculate about events that you don't clearly remember.

> **Important!**
> **Don't be afraid of the words,**
> **"I don't know" or "I don't remember."**

Frighteningly, even those aspects of the event that you believe you clearly remember might still be the product of confabulation, because memory is never a true mechanical recording of the external world.[26] This is one reason (among many others) that savvy trial lawyers urge their clients not to give statements in the immediate aftermath, nor to speak with the police without legal counsel.

Denial response

One of the hardest things I ever did was to tell one of my best friends that her son had just been airlifted to a major trauma center following a major rollover accident. She immediately gasped, "NO! No, no, no... he can't have!" That's a denial response. Because we are verbal creatures, the normal human reaction to an overwhelming negative input is a verbal denial.

In the immediate aftermath of a shooting, you may be so horrified by the event – by the criminal's assault on you, by the horrific nature of what happens when a chunk of fast-moving lead impacts a soft human body, by your knowledge of what the event will mean for your family in the days to come – that your unattended mouth may try to deny what happened or to disclaim your own deliberate actions.[27] This is yet another reason to avoid giving a statement immediately after a shooting.

26-In one study, 21 percent of law enforcement officers involved in critical encounters reported that they "saw, heard, or experienced something during the event that I later found out had not really happened." See *Perceptual and Memory Distortion* (2002).

27-A deliberate and intentional shooting may be defensible in court, but an unintentional shooting almost never is. A denial response on the scene can most definitely come back to bite you later.

Mindset as the determining survival factor

During his LFI-2 classes, Massad Ayoob shows students a video interview of an amazing young survivor. Stacy Lim, an officer from the Los Angeles Police Department, pulled into her driveway late one night. She was not in uniform, as she had been visiting friends. Unknown to her, she had been followed home by a group of gangbangers with the intent of committing a carjacking. When she stepped out of her truck, she was almost immediately shot in the chest at close range with a .357 Magnum round which penetrated her heart and blew a tennis ball-sized exit wound out her back. "I was pissed," she reported. "Just really pissed." She proceeded to return fire, chasing her attacker to the back of her truck as she defended herself. The remaining attackers fled the scene. After she dealt with the attackers, she headed toward her home to call for help, but passed out before she got there. Her attacker died, and she lived to return to patrol duty eight months later. "You need to prepare your mind for where your body may have to go," she asserts today. Although she was the victim of a surprise attack with severe injuries – shot through the heart with a .357 Magnum! – she lived because she was mentally prepared to stay in the fight and because she simply *refused* to lose.[28]

In Lt. Col. Dave Grossman's excellent book, *On Combat*, he asserts, "I know of gangbangers who have sucked up a dozen 9mm rounds and drove on to survive. If they can do it, you can too.... I know of a little old lady who was stabbed 20 times and

---

28- Lim's story is told in multiple books, as she has understandably become something of a legend in the law enforcement world. See *On Combat*, p 144-145 and *Into the Kill Zone*, p 116-121 (she is not identified by name in the latter volume, in keeping with the terms of the grant which funded the study upon which the book is based). If you have the opportunity to take an LFI-2 class, you may be fortunate enough to view a videotaped speech Stacy Lim gave to an LFI class several years ago.

then crawled to the phone, dialed 9-1-1, and lived to tell about it. Never, ever give up after being shot or stabbed. Do not train yourself to die and do not train other warriors to die."[29]

Urey W. Patrick and John C. Hall, in their book *In Defense of Self and Others*, tell us, "Personal determination to survive is a significant factor affecting the ultimate survival chances of the individual. It is a factor that must be instructed .... The simple truth to be driven home is that just because you are injured, you don't have to die."[30]

Mindset is everything. If you are injured, *keep going*. Don't give up. Don't quit. Keep going until you have prevailed. If your attacker is still active, put him down. Stop him from hitting you with another bullet; stop him from stabbing or striking you again. Do whatever it takes to stop him from harming you further.

When you have vanquished your attacker, whether he has run away or fallen to the ground either dead or unconscious, *don't you quit yet!* Your next mission is to get yourself to medical attention. Crawl, walk, wriggle, run, writhe, or drive to medical support.[31] No matter how bad your injuries might appear, you can still function. You can still call for help.

If you are alive enough to know that you were hit, you are alive enough to *choose* survival.

Summary

This chapter has provided a very brief and necessarily simplistic picture of some types of reactions a human body and mind can experience under stress. It's important to note that almost nobody will experience *all* such reactions, but nearly everyone will

29-Dave Grossman, *On Combat*, p 133.
30-Urey W. Patrick and John C. Hall, *In Defense of Self and Others...: Issues, Facts & Fallacies-The Realities Of Law Enforcement's Use Of Deadly Force*. Carolina Academic Press, 2005, p 67.
31-Dave Grossman, *On Combat*, p145.

experience *some* of them.[32] There is some evidence that memory distortions are not just common, but nearly inevitable.[33] Further, there are other reactions closely related to the above that we haven't had time to touch on here. As noted researcher Dr. Alexis Artwohl observes, "There is virtually no factor in a shooting that can't be subject to perceptual or memory distortion."[34]

The human brain is a complex, complicated mechanism, and human beings are all individuals. Everyone experiences life just a little differently from everyone else, and processes information differently too. We can make some broad generalizations about the types of perceptual distortions or anomalies a person might experience during a life-threatening event, but every individual is just that, an individual. The important thing to remember here is that if you experience one or more of the sensations listed above, or any other perceptual anomaly, *it doesn't mean something is wrong*. It means that something is very, very right: your body and brain have become physically prepared to fight hard and WIN.

32-*Perceptual and Memory Distortions* (2008), pgs 19-3 through 19-4, and related tables. Across the various studies, estimates typically run at 90 percent to 95 percent of participants experiencing one or more of the tracked perceptual distortions.
33-*Critical Incident Amnesia*, p 1.
34-*Perceptual and Memory Distortions* (2008), p 19-6.

Chapter 9 - On a Cold February Night

Mark Walters

"I agree 100% having been through a stalking situation ourselves; my wife and I learned some very valuable lessons. We sought and received a full order of protection from the courts. In my opinion, the paper was completely useless. Our attacker violated this order numerous times and yet the local Sheriff Department couldn't find this freak. He lived about a half mile from our house and despite my seeing him twice a day and doing as the Phelps County Sheriff Department suggested ('Do not approach/confront...let us do our jobs.'), he never was apprehended. He continued to stalk, peek in our windows and threaten us. Each time we reported...same result...nothing! After pleading with law enforcement to do something... anything, on a cold February night it all came to an end!"

The above post appeared in the USCCA discussion forum on 8/20/2008. The thread was titled: *"What do you do about a stalker?"* I placed a call to the writer, Mr. Jim Butler. My interview with Mr. Butler sent chills up my back. The Butlers' account of terror is something no human beings should have to go through. Jim and his wife, Suzanne, have allowed me to pass their story on to you. Read it carefully and more importantly, learn from it.

February, 2003: the nightmare begins

"We started having problems with a neighbor. My wife didn't notify me at first. She caught him peeking in windows and she didn't want me to have too bad a reaction to that, I suppose," Jim told me as our discussion began. "When I first became aware of what was happening, I was on a business trip in California when I got a phone call around 2 am. My wife had caught him peeking in a window again and called the Phelps County Sheriff. They didn't see him at first and when they came back they were able to spot him. That's the night that it started. That was in February of 2003."

The neighbor was 44 year old David Brown. Jim told me, "He lived in a trailer on his sister's property about a half a mile from us. He didn't have any electricity or running water and lived kind of like a hermit. We took a little bit of pity on him because he obviously didn't have any money or anything. We offered him small odd jobs around our place, cutting grass, feeding our horses when we were out of town, things like that."

After being spotted by deputies that evening while Jim was in California, David Brown barricaded himself in his trailer. This resulted in a SWAT response from local authorities. During the standoff Brown armed himself, threatened deputies, and refused to exit his residence alive. After nearly two hours, a county sheriff hostage negotiator persuaded him to come out without violence. He was taken for psychiatric evaluation and found to be mentally fit. Brown was later charged with first degree trespassing and resisting arrest.

Little did the Butlers know what had really begun for them on that February night in 2003.

Summer of harassment

As the harassment began after Jim returned home from California, the Butlers' lives were never "normal" again. "We're doing everything we can legally, to keep him away from the house," Jim said. Suzanne applied for a protective injunction within 24 hours of the first incident, which the courts granted immediately.

"Occurrences of him coming around, though, did not stop. In fact I confronted him one time in front of the house," Jim told me. "Apparently he was coming into the house when we weren't there, and he would take a handful of change, grab a couple of beers out of the refrigerator," Jim said. "He would never take anything like a stereo or TV and I really had no proof he was there other than the little stuff like that. I suspect he gained access by the garage door opener. He must have had the code and I have no idea how many times he may have entered the house."

Throughout the spring and summer and into the fall, the harassment of the Butlers became regular and frequent. Each time it happened, the Butlers made a report to law enforcement. Jim told me that the county sheriff was called to his property at least every two to three weeks to make another report about Brown's activities.

The Butlers would hear loud cars pass by with the occupants shouting obscenities, as well as occasional gunfire from passing vehicles. Their frustration levels rose as they spent many months trying to get this man arrested while it seemed as if nothing was being done by local law enforcement to prevent David Brown from repeatedly violating the injunctions against him.

Merry Christmas

There were repeated violations during the ten months following the February incident, but still no arrest. The couple lived in a constant state of alert when home, cautiously waiting and listening, and remaining armed at all times both inside and outside. Jim and his wife began spending more time training with their firearms. Both purchased new guns: Jim a Glock 21, and Suzanne a Glock 19. Having grown up in St. Louis, Suzanne was not familiar with firearms, but she now spent a significant amount of time training with her husband. Jim told me that part of this was by design, so that the neighbors would hear the gunfire coming from their property as a form of deterrence. It didn't work.

On Christmas Eve, 2003, Jim was heading towards the house when Suzanne called. She had beaten him home by just a few minutes. As she exited her vehicle she noticed flashlight beams inside the house. A moment later, she was confronted by David Brown as he exited her home. A scuffle ensued and Suzanne was injured. Brown escaped into the darkness. Phelps County Sheriff's officers responded in conjunction with the Missouri State Highway Patrol, and charges were drafted against Brown. The home was dusted for prints, and the Butlers gave statements. Brown was not apprehended that evening, but now had four warrants for his arrest.

Angered and enraged by the apparent ability of David Brown to elude capture, and frustrated by what appeared to be a lack of effort by the sheriff's department, the Butlers were prepared to handle Brown themselves if necessary. The authorities would later determine that David Brown's sister had been using a police scanner to warn her brother of attempts to find him.

February, 2004 - the end

David Brown seemingly disappeared for a while. "He knew he was in trouble now," Jim said. "His court dates were coming up and we didn't see him for a while. As my frustration grew, I made repeated trips to the sheriff's department to tell the captain that this had to stop, that this was going somewhere I don't want it to go. I don't want to get hurt, I definitely don't want to hurt anyone, but this has to stop. I'm worried for my safety. I don't know if someone is going to take a shot at me from the woods or someplace." Jim was informed that he had the right to defend himself in his home and "all that nonsense."

"Now I start seeing him (David Brown) again and each time I see him I call and report him," Jim said, "yet he was still never picked up."

It's now February 4, one full year from the initial encounter. Upon arriving home from work, Jim and Suzanne see what appears to be a large party at David Brown's sister's house. Arming themselves, they watch intently throughout the evening, but the Butlers have no idea what is about to happen.

Jim later told me, "It's a very bitter, cold night. It gets to be about 11 o'clock. I said, 'Honey, I don't think anything is going to happen. I'm going to bed.'" Jim went to bed and fell asleep while Suzanne worked in the kitchen on the computer. He continues, "I was asleep and Suzanne had just came to bed. He [Brown] was obviously watching for that moment we both went to bed so he could catch us both in bed. He kicked in the door and took about two to three steps and shot me in the neck while I slept."

The bullet wound to Jim's neck grazed near his artery but didn't sever it. Jim told me, "As I sat up then he shot me with a rifle in the chest." Jim rolled toward the nightstand to grab his gun while Suzanne, unaware of whether her husband was alive or dead, in an act of total heroism sprung forward, rushed to the bedroom, and grabbed the rifle barrel from the madman standing at the foot of her bed who was hellbent on killing her husband.

During the struggle that ensued, Suzanne was subsequently shot in the hand and in the wrist, with the shot to her wrist exiting near her elbow. "Despite being shot twice, she doesn't let go of the rifle. She doesn't know my condition, and they are struggling over the gun. I began screaming and fired four times above them to get them to separate. As soon as I got enough separation and I could shoot, I did. I unloaded the rest of the magazine at him," Jim recalls. "I emptied the first magazine, reloaded and fired two more shots."

David Brown hit the floor with a thud and, unbeknownst to the Butlers, died within seconds.

"HE SHOT ME, HE SHOT ME," Suzanne was screaming. Jim then sprang from the bed to his wife. "Honestly, I didn't even know I was shot. I can't really describe it. I wasn't sure if he was going to spring up so I kept going back to make sure he was still down. I don't know how many times I went back to the room to check on him, maybe three or four times. I go into the rest of the house and turn on all the lights."

After the gunfight Suzanne left the room immediately to call 911.

Actual 911 transcript:

Emergency 911: "Emergency 911."

Suzanne Butler: "I've been shot!"

Emergency 911: "You've been shot?"

Suzanne Butler: "Yes, me and my husband!"

Emergency 911: "How many people have been shot?"

Jim Butler: "My wife, myself and him, he's laying on the floor!"

Emergency 911: "Where is she hit?"

Jim Butler: "She is hit in the arm!"

Emergency 911: "What about the guy lying on the floor?"

Jim Butler: "I think he's dead!"

The couple, now hysterical, waited for authorities to arrive. Not knowing who might show up from the party down the street, Jim refused to put his gun down when he heard someone come up behind him.

"Drop the weapon!" commanded the first responding officer. Refusing to comply with the officer's request until he was certain he and his wife were safe, Jim refused to lay down his sidearm. The officer never drew his weapon on Jim. "At this point you don't know who's on your side," Jim said later. After several tense moments, Jim set the gun down on a nearby table.

As the house filled with emergency personnel and law enforcement, the dead man's sister, Jane Helgersen, made an attempt to rush into the home. She was immediately tackled by authorities and charged with hindering prosecution and resisting arrest.

The Butlers were taken to Phelps County Regional Medical Center and released within 24 hours. In addition to the two gunshot wounds he received, Jim also suffered a broken ankle during the gunfight. The bullet fired into his chest resides there to this day.

David W. Brown received four shots to the upper body including right shoulder, upper chest, right chest, and right lower chest. According to the autopsy report, all four shots produced mortal wounds.

In addition to the Ruger 10-22 rifle with which he shot the Butlers, Brown was carrying 75 rounds of ammunition in his pockets, a .22 handgun, and a fanny pack which contained latex gloves and additional ammunition. Police would later surmise that he intended to murder the Butlers and then commit suicide. Why would someone determined to kill themselves carry latex gloves obviously meant to hide fingerprints? Fortunately, we will never know the entire story of what this man intended to do.

Jim and Suzanne Butler stayed with relatives for the next month, going home daily to retrieve the mail and check on the property. They have since moved back into their home with a certain feeling of cautious relief as the home invader's family still reside down the street. Other than some hard stares and occasional horn blaring, the couple has been free of harassment.

Chapter 10 - Stalking and Stalkers

Kathy Jackson

As the Butlers discovered, dealing with a stalker can be difficult business.

What is stalking?

The exact legal definition of stalking varies from state to state, but all 50 states have enacted legislation which specifically and directly criminalizes stalking. And all states have laws against many of the specific behaviors common to stalkers.[1]

For our purposes, stalking is *a repeated and ongoing pattern of behavior which would lead a reasonable person to conclude that the perpetrator intended to frighten, harass, or terrify the victim*.[2]

Stalking may include (but is not limited to) the following behaviors:

- *Gifts and notes*. These unwanted items can range from the simple to the extravagant, from the bizarre to the frightening. They can be outwardly pleasant, sexually oriented, outright threatening, or simply off-the-wall – and

---

1-For information about specific stalking laws in individual states, see the Stalking Resource Center from the National Center for Victims of crime online at http://www.ncvc.org (accessed January 2009).

2-Throughout this chapter I will be using the word "victim" to denote the target of the stalker's activity. We all realize that the politically sensitive word would be "survivor," but the difficulty in a stalking case is that stalking is an *ongoing situation* rather than a one-time event.

everything in between. (For those inclined to read this description and wonder *what's so bad about a gift?*, one typical and real-life example of a male stalker's "gift" to a female victim would be a used condom draped over her doorknob every morning.)

• *Vandalism*. Again, this can range from petty to serious, and may even include dangerous violent crimes such as arson of a home in which people are sleeping. Some stalkers slash tires; others engage in petty behavior like smearing Vaseline on the victim's car window every night, or repeatedly knocking over the victim's mailbox during the day.

• *Surveillance*. Stalkers are masters of tracking their victims and recording what they observe. They peep through windows, park outside the victim's home to observe her comings and goings, hire private detective agencies, or even root through the victim's trash to gather information about the victim's life. Some of the information they learn may show up later in threatening phone calls or notes. Other tidbits may be kept in a journal or diary in the stalker's home. Some stalkers even publish their detailed observations of the victim via email or internet pages.

• *Constant communication*. Obsessive phone calls and a copious number of emails or text messages are not uncommon. It's not unheard-of for a stalker to dial the victim's home number over and over and over again, and to persist doing so for hours or even days without a break.

• *"Trophy" collection*. Some folks would call this petty thievery. The stalker breaks in, takes some minor but meaningful item, and leaves without disturbing anything else. Frequently targeted: underwear or night clothing, photo albums, mementos that are significant to the stalker and perhaps to the victim as well (a matchbook, if the initial encounter took place in a nightclub, for example).

• ***Harassment and other nuisance tactics***, including legal suits, unwanted contact with the victim's family and friends, ordering useless magazine subscriptions or cancelling utility services in the victim's name, attempts to get the victim fired from work, and libel or slander.

• ***Violence or threats of violence***. It's important to note that not all stalkers progress to violence, though stalking behavior does tend to worsen over time (and almost *never* improves spontaneously). Crucial: some stalkers are violent without threatening, others threaten without committing violence. And some, of course, do both.

In addition, *any* ongoing pattern of behavior apparently intended to – or which in fact does – intimidate, frighten, or coerce the victim very likely falls under the legal definition of stalking in most states.

Prevalence of stalking

How common is it? Studies have shown that around 7% of women, and around 2% of men in the United States, report being stalked at some point during their lifetimes.[3]

Who stalks?

Although stalking can be perpetrated by a person of either sex, and the stalker may choose a victim of either sex, the majority of stalkers are male and the majority of stalking victims are female. *But this is not always the case*. The crime itself is gender-neutral. Male stalkers may select either male or female victims, and female stalkers may select either male or female

3-Basile, K. C., Swahn, M. H., Chen, J., & Saltzman, L. E. (2006). *Stalking in the United States: Recent national prevalence estimates*. American Journal of Preventive Medicine, 31, 172-175.

victims. If you are involved in a stalking situation which is an exception to the general rule, the danger can be just as real as the danger in situations which fit the more common pattern.

Because of the common demographics in stalking cases, for clarity's sake throughout this chapter, I've generally used "he" to refer to the stalker and "she" to refer to the victim. However, be aware that this language is not intended to lessen, denigrate, belittle or deny either the reality or the danger of situations where the stalker is a "she" or the victim a "he." Although male stalkers are more common and are statistically more likely to engage in violence, *any individual female stalker can be just as dangerous as a male stalker, and should be taken every bit as seriously.*

There are different ways to classify stalking cases. Many investigators prefer to use a simple, relationship-based rule:

- *Domestic violence stalkers*. These are those who have previously had an intimate relationship with their victims. Some people speak with uneasy amusement of having a "psycho ex," a former spouse or intimate friend who just doesn't seem to understand that the relationship is over, and who reacts in inappropriate and frightening ways to the loss. Other times, the stalking behavior actually starts while the relationship is still intact: one partner becomes increasingly possessive and controlling as time goes on, and eventually crosses the line into outright abuse from which the victim cannot seem to escape.

- *Acquaintance stalkers*. In these cases, the victim recognizes the stalker, but they never lived together or had an intimate relationship. If they dated, it was casual rather than serious. This type of stalker isn't as common as the domestic violence variety, but such people are still out there and can be dangerous. This category includes most varieties of workplace stalking.

• ***Stranger stalkers.*** Although perhaps most frightening, this is the least common type of stalker. Some of these, perhaps the majority, may be termed "celebrity stalkers." These people choose a public figure such as a television or film star, or a radio personality, to fixate upon. Unfortunately, you needn't be a celebrity to pick up this type of stalker. Simply being in the public eye, however tangentially, can put you at risk. If you regularly give public presentations, or if your name and face appears on company literature, or if you volunteer as a spokesperson for a local non-profit agency, you might be a "celebrity" to some deluded soul.

Stalkers typically progress through the following stages:

• ***"I want you to love me."*** In this phase, the stalker fixates on the victim, often for reasons initially known only to him. He may court the victim – sometimes successfully, sometimes not. In some cases, the stalker is suffering under the delusion that the victim does, in fact, love him, even if the opposite is true or even if the victim has never met the stalker. It is this phase which often causes victims to feel guilty after the fact, wondering what they did to attract the stalker's attentions, or castigating themselves for falling for his ploy and giving him some of the attention he demanded. But stalking behavior has very little to do with the victim's initial actions, and everything to do with the stalker's twisted emotional landscape.[4]

• ***"You MUST love me."*** The stalker's behavior turns

4-Please note that the "I want you to love me" stage does not necessarily refer to romantic love. It might instead be displayed in the desperate attempts of an undesirable job applicant to get hired despite her lack of qualifications, or by any number of other similar situations where the (potential) victim has something or represents something the stalker wants.

possessive and takes on a frightening undertone.

- *"If I can't have you, nobody can."* The stalker's behavior becomes overtly negative, dangerous and threatening.

Some stalkers apparently skip straight over the faux "love" stage and progress directly to resentment or naked hate. Again, this can be for reasons known only to the stalker, and has very little to do with the victim's actions.

Assessing the danger

Stalking ends in the victim's murder less than 2% of the time;[5] not often, but certainly often enough to be wary. And the low number of actual killings is no consolation whatsoever to the murdered victims and their families. In addition, in approximately 20% of stalking cases, the victim reports a physical assault; the stalker uses a weapon such as a gun or a knife in roughly 4% of those incidents.[6]

The following circumstances *may* increase the likelihood of a violent outcome:

- the stalker is male
- the stalker abuses drugs or alcohol
- the stalker has been violent in the past, even if that violence was not directed toward the stalking victim
- the stalker has a criminal record
- the victim and the stalker have had an intimate relationship; in these cases, the danger is typically highest during the time frame immediately surrounding the break-up
- the stalker is unemployed or socially isolated
- the stalker has threatened suicide, murder, or both

5-*Stalking and Serious Violence.* David V. James, MA, MB, BS, and Frank R. Farnham, MB, BS. J Am Acad Psychiatry Law 31:432–9, 2003
6-*National Crime Victimization Survey: Stalking Victimization in the United States.* By Katrina Baum, Ph.D., Shannan Catalano, Ph.D., and Michael Rand of the Bureau of Justice Statistics; and Kristina Rose of the National Institute of Justice. Available online on the BJS World Wide Web Internet site at **www.ojp.usdoj. gov/bjs/abstract/svus.htm.**

• the stalker has an untreated mental health issue[7]

Lessening the risk

To lower (not eliminate) the risk of picking up a stalker in the first place, the most important tip I can give you is to trust your gut. When you encounter someone who sets off the internal alarms which are nature's early-warning system, don't ignore the claxon noise. Heed it, and steer clear of any involvement with that person – no matter how charming they might otherwise be, and no matter how inconvenient it will be to do so.

Always remember that "No" is a complete sentence. If your intuition tells you this person is dangerous or 'has issues,' don't soften the no! Don't tell the person seeking a date, "I'm in a relationship now..." or "Now is not a good time for me." Don't tell the person seeking a handyman job, "We don't need anyone to do yardwork right now." Where a normal person might hear these statements and realize he should go elsewhere, a person prone to stalking behavior hears these words as implying that now isn't a good time, but later might be. He hears, "Come back tomorrow."

If you have a job that puts you in front of the public in any way, be especially protective of your private information. While you may not be able to limit the appearance of your name or photograph in public, you can and should limit others' knowledge of your home address, your personal phone numbers, and similar data. Use a PO box for your mail, get an unlisted number, and pay special attention to avoiding identity theft.

Those who enjoy spending time online should be especially wary of confiding personal information to strangers they meet

7-*Stalking and Serious Violence*. David V. James, MA, MB, BS, and Frank R. Farnham, MB, BS. J Am Acad Psychiatry Law 31:432–9, 2003

there.[8] It's tempting to think that those we have met only online 'know' us, or we 'know' them. In reality, online interaction is startlingly poor at providing the rich context of behavioral cues that allow most of us to filter the nutcases from the sane in personal life. Be especially wary of trusting online acquaintances with personal data.

If you are being stalked: things to do

First and most important: take the situation seriously. While denial may be tempting, it is not productive. Do everything within your power to lessen your risk, and be prepared to physically defend yourself if necessary.

Be aware of the world around you. Try to maintain a state of relaxed alertness at all times, noticing other people and what they are doing as you go about your business. This is your early-warning system to avoid trouble!

Improve home security by getting better locks on your doors and windows, beefing up lighting outside the home, and drawing your curtains so outsiders cannot see in.

Protect your personal information just as you would against any type of identity theft.[9] If your stalker does not already know where you live, or if you are a public figure and want to lessen the chances of picking up a stalker in the first place, avoid giving out your home address to *any person* or *any organization*. Get an unlisted phone number, and use a PO box rather than having mail delivered to your doorstep. What others do not know, they cannot inadvertently spill to the wrong person.

8-Ahh, the internet! Where the men are men, the women are men, and the children are FBI agents.

9-A quick internet search for "identity theft" or "identity theft prevention" will turn up thousands of websites dedicated to providing good, up-to-the-minute strategies for defeating identity theft. Most if not all of these techniques will work equally well for denying information to the stalker as they will for defeating the more ordinary type of thief.

Watch what you throw away. Receipts, bill stubs, credit card solicitations, and other, similar items may all contain personal information you don't want the stalker to know. *Thoroughly* destroy these items, perhaps with a shredder, before placing them in the trash.

Tell your family and friends what is happening. Remember: even if you were involved with the stalker in some way in the past, his stalking behavior is *not your fault*. Your family and your friends need to know about the situation so they can help you protect your privacy. Additionally, as long as you keep the situation to yourself, that bottled-up secret will have a life of its own, and keeping the secret can be just one more way the stalker has power over you. Spill the beans, and you're free of at least *that* worry.

Contact your local law enforcement agency for help solving the long-term problem, but *don't expect them to keep you safe* in the meanwhile. Keeping you safe is not their job! Their job is to investigate and solve crimes after the fact, hopefully gathering enough evidence to put the criminal in jail and keep him there. Your job is to survive the crime in the first place. As Lyn Bates writes in her book, *Safety for Stalking Victims*, "Safety is what you need, and you can get it! It is almost entirely in your control! 'Justice,' on the other hand, is mostly under the control of other people, which is why you cannot always get it."

Keep good records of what happened, when it happened, and how it happened.[10] Record phone calls and other encounters. Get immediate statements from people who witness any threatening activity from your stalker. Take pictures of vandalism and other property crimes. Keep a simple log of events,

10-*Safety for Stalking Victims: how to save your privacy, your sanity, and your life*. Lyn Bates. Writer's Showcase, 2001. ISBN 0-595-18160-0. p. xxiv

recording what happened, where it happened, and the names of any witnesses, along with a written note recording what you did in response to the behavior. Gather evidence and keep it in a safe place, presenting it to the authorities as needed.

Call in all the people you think may be able to help – the cops, a lawyer, the local crisis center, friends and family – and then be prepared to give each of these folks the ammunition they need in order to help you. As unfair as it seems, *you are the only person who will witness every single thing the stalker does against you* and that means *you* are your own best witness for making a criminal case against him.

Contact the local women's crisis center and follow their recommendations. There's a whole world of resources out there to help people cope with this kind of problem, and it's downright foolish not to use such resources.

Speaking of resources, if you are being stalked by someone with whom you share custody or visitation rights for a minor child, there's a nasty little secret that stalkers hate: in many locales, it's possible to use your local law enforcement agency as a pick up and drop off point. It works like this: you bring the child in to the station and leave the child under the watchful eye of a law enforcement officer designated for this duty. The other parent then arrives and picks up the child, without seeing you or having any contact with you in any way. At the end of the visitation time, the other party returns the child(ren) to the station and leaves before you arrive. If you are serious about avoiding contact with the stalker, it's a very smart move. And as a side effect, it allows local police to become familiar with your family and situation – a bonus for those being stalked and a bane for the stalker.

If you are being stalked: things to avoid

First and most important: ***Don't try to handle it entirely by yourself***. As self-defense expert Marc MacYoung says: "Bottom line here, if the guy

- didn't already know he could take you
- was afraid of you and what you can do, and
- wasn't pretty sure he could get away with it –

HE WOULDN'T BE DOING IT IN THE FIRST PLACE!" [11]

Put another way, "Stalkers are like bullies in that they specialize in picking on people who won't call for help – for whatever reason."[12]

Don't assume that anyone else can or will protect you. You will need help from other people in order to put the offender behind bars and stop the stalking, and you also need the emotional and physical help provided by alert friends and caring family members, but always remember that nobody else will have more interest in protecting you than you do yourself. This is not a job you can hand off to another person and forget about!

Don't engage in denial. It's unfair, it sucks, and it is what it is. You have a stalker and your life has changed.

"*Don't inadvertently [reward] the stalker's behavior* by having some contact with him, such as finally picking up the phone after he has called you 50 times and gotten your answering machine, or answering the door after the 100th time he rang your doorbell. You just taught him that it takes at least 50 calls or 100 rings to get in touch with you, and next time he'll gladly

11-Marc MacYoung on the No Nonsense Self Defense website, http://www.non-onsenseselfdefense.com/stalking.html, accessed 1/24/09
12- Marc MacYoung on the No Nonsense Self Defense website, http://www.non-onsenseselfdefense.com/stalkingsolutions.htm, accessed 1/24/09

try even harder, maybe 100 phone calls or 200 doorbell-rings," writes Lyn Bates, in her book *Safety for Stalking Victims*.[13]

Don't contact the stalker. He might be charming, apologetic, friendly, helpful – fill in your own adjective – 95% of the time, but that other 5% can kill you. Don't get fooled! Keep your distance.

Building a safety plan

It's important to include this disclaimer with the ideas below: although these suggestions about how to prevent or defend oneself against stalking have worked for others in the past, *they aren't always going to work every time in every situation.* There are plenty of variables in any given set of circumstances, and real life is often messy enough to defy simple rules-of-thumb. If you believe you are currently in danger from a stalker, contact your local law enforcement agency and work with them concerning your circumstances. Also note the resources available in the footnotes at the end of this chapter. They barely scratch the surface of what is available to those whose lives are affected by stalking behavior.

If you or someone you love is being stalked, you need to develop some basic plans for how to deal with situations that could predictably come up.

During the course of a typical day you can predict that you will spend time at home, in your car (perhaps driving a specific route to work), at your place of employment, perhaps the grocery store or shopping mall, and then home again. You might also eat at a favored restaurant, or drop in to visit the home of one of your friends. Each of these locations presents a unique set of circumstances, but *the number of locations is finite.* Always

13-Bates, *Safety for Stalking Victims*, p. 184

remember there are a limited number of places your stalker might find you – and that it is quite possible to come up with a contingency plan for dealing with an encounter in each one. If you have a plan in mind for a given location, you'll be much more prepared to defend yourself and survive if an attack does happen in that location.

For each place you spend time, you'll need to know the location of

- doors, windows, and alternate exit routes from the building. Always be aware that these can also be *entry* routes for the stalker.
- the nearest landline telephone, which is better than a cell phone for calling 911 as it is more likely to give the 911 operator the correct address.
- the most likely place you can immediately find other people if the stalker enters the area.
- the closest, best place to shelter and prepare to physically defend yourself if you cannot make an immediate exit.

Please note this doesn't mean you'll have to limit yourself to these known locations! Far from it. Once you've gotten in the habit of noticing details in familiar locations, such as where doors and windows are located, where the nearest telephone is, or a location within the building where you might shelter and prepare to physically defend yourself if necessary, you'll find that this awareness often carries over to prod you to look for these important factors whenever you enter an unfamiliar location too.

This type of relaxed alertness, knowing where you would go and what you would do if attacked, will serve you well whether or not you are currently being stalked. For someone who *is* being stalked, however, it's absolutely vital.

Restraining orders

A restraining order helps you establish a paper trail of offenses. It gives police what they need in order to arrest the stalker. It gives the DA what he or she needs in order to bring charges against the stalker. And it gives the jury the information they need in order to convict the stalker.

But *that's all it does*.

It does not keep the stalker away from you. It does not lock your doors or bar your windows. It does not physically protect you from any sort of attack. And even if the restraining order *could* keep you physically safer, the fact is that in stalking cases, approximately 80% of all restraining orders are violated.[14],[15]

A restraining order may lead to an arrest, a charge, and – if things go right – a conviction with serious jail time. All of these are desirable, but not one of them will keep you safe. *Your choices* and *your actions* will keep you safe. A piece of paper will not.

Dealing with police in an ongoing situation

Here are some tips about how to maintain your good-guy status *and* your sanity.

First, get the restraining order. As mentioned above, this is a necessary tool that will open up a lot of options for people within the justice system to help you. Refusal to get the restrain-

---

14-*Stalking in America: Findings From the National Violence Against Women Survey*. Patricia Tjaden and Nancy Thoennes, April 1998. The full report is available from the National Criminal Justice Reference Service at: http://www.ncjrs.org/txtfiles/169592.txt
15-While initially alarming, this statistic may be reassuring to those who note that a stalking offense which would otherwise be treated as a misdemeanor in some jurisdictions will usually become a felony if a violated restraining order is involved.

ing order really ties the hands of the responding officers and limits them to actions which are very likely to enrage the stalker without accomplishing anything worthwhile.

If you do get a restraining order, *abide by it*. Police officers are often jaded about these types of cases because the most common pattern of behavior is for the victim to call the cops, the cops arrive and separate the parties, maybe haul the perpetrator off to jail for the weekend, victim gets a restraining order, perp gets out of jail – and the next thing you know, perp is over at the victim's *house at the victim's invitation* and the cycle starts all over again. For this reason, cops may initially be suspicious of your sincerity when you obtain that piece of paper. But you still need the paper, and your willingness to follow the restrictions upon it even when the restrictions have an effect on your life is the best proof of sincerity you can give law enforcement officers. Once they realize you're serious and not typical, they'll be a lot more willing to go the extra mile to solve your case.

Never cry wolf. Remember that if your stalker (for example) drives a little red import, not *all* little red imports that pull up behind you and tailgate will be driven by the stalker. Be sure of the sighting before you report it.

Always remember that the individual law enforcement officers you are dealing with do not have ultimate power over the outcome of the case. Interacting with these officers may be encouraging or discouraging, positive or negative. But they are on your side against the forces of evil, and *they don't know what is going to happen in the courts any better than you do!* Don't hold it against the individual officer if and when things go wrong. No matter how frustrated you might become, remember that the individual officer is an ally, not an enemy, and that you very likely will need a good working relationship with that officer and the other officers in the same department if and when the stalker returns.

Finally, keep good records. When did the stalker last contact you? What, exactly, did he say or do? What was your response? Who else witnessed the behavior? The answers to these questions – recorded in a concrete, permanent format – really help build your case.

As the Butlers learned to their sorrow, this type of information may help the case within the justice system (and thus you need to have it), but like the restraining order itself, it's not going to do anything in terms of keeping you safe. Your actions keep you safe. Paper trails, even necessary paper trails, do not.

Some resources for stalking victims

AWARE
PO Box 242
Bedford MA 01730-0242
877-672-9273
www.AWARE.org

How to Stop a Stalker
by Mike Proctor
Published by Prometheus Books, 2003
ISBN 978-1591020912

No Nonsense Self Defense
www.nononsenseselfdefense.com

The link above is to Marc MacYoung and Dianna Gordon MacYoung's website about self defense. They have a sensible and worthwhile approach to stalking and related issues. Be sure to check out the "Pyramid of Safety" and the "Five Stages of Violent Crime" articles.

Safety for Stalking Victims: How to save your privacy, your sanity, and your life
by Lyn Bates
Published by iUniverse, 2001
ISBN 978-0595181605

Chapter 11 - A Cold Day in Hell

Mark Walters

Meet Marco Ricaldone, a North Miami, Florida licensed paramedic and all around nice guy. By all accounts he is a hero, a lifesaver, one of the folks who come to our aid when we need it most. Working throughout the night when most of us are fast asleep, Marco is the man who shows up to help us in our darkest hour. When you are desperate for life-saving assistance it is Marco and his colleagues who you can count on for help.

By the very nature of his chosen field, he is dedicated to the preservation of life, and has dedicated himself to helping others in need. A hero indeed. At 28 years old, Marco is beyond his years in compassion, and it shone through during our conversations, some of which were pierced by the wailing sirens of his vehicle as he rushed to someone's aid. He is also a man who has been tested. Having administered aid to the victims of senseless crimes and tended to the fallen victims of gunfire on the mean streets of Miami, he never believed he would one day be forced to fire a weapon in his own act of self-preservation.

I had spoken to Marco several times prior to arranging our formal interview and was aware of the outline of events that transpired on January 13, 2008. As usual, I became spellbound by the details as they emerged during our sometimes graphic discussion.

Every Wednesday on his night off, Marco would relax and share the camaraderie of friends and fellow car enthusiasts as a member of a local Volkswagen-Audi car club. It was a relief from working the tough and often inhospitable streets of Miami. During his weekly meetings, Marco befriended a young lady and her husband: Jennifer and Emanuel. After about two months, Jennifer showed up to one of the club meetings without her husband. She informed Marco that her relationship with Emanuel had deteriorated and that the couple had separated and filed for divorce. After exchanging phone numbers, Marco and Jennifer began communicating outside of the gatherings and enjoying time together. One day the text messages and harassment began. Their movie outings were frequently interrupted by harassing cell phone calls and continual text messages. "I know where you are," said the menacing texts as the cell phone alerted another message. "It will be a cold day in hell before the two of you are together."

Marco told me, "Her husband worked with computers and would follow her by tracking her expenditures online. He knew where we were. I began to realize this guy was crazy. I started receiving threatening text messages like, 'Stay away from her or you're dead.' He would get drunk and send threats, then apologize when he was sober saying things like 'I would never do anything like that.'"

It seemed that cars were not Emanuel's only passion, and it was confirmed by Jennifer that Emanuel owned firearms. "I found out he had around 17 guns or something like that," Marco told me. He continued, "Whenever we were together the messages and calls would come in. I had never been a gun owner, a handgun anyway. I had always wanted a pistol and this seemed like the right time, so I headed out to Bass Pro Shop and purchased a Springfield XD, took it to the range and loved it. I began keeping my new gun loaded on the nightstand in case this guy ever decided to show up."

As the threats showed no signs of subsiding, Marco began asking Jennifer to stay at his house. He later informed me that "her parents never locked the doors and what was happening just didn't seem to bother them."

They found out that Emanuel had recently quit his job for no apparent reason. Marco told me, "I knew when I found out he had quit his job that something was wrong. This guy wasn't right." Taking him up on his offer that Friday evening, Jennifer agreed to spend the night for her own safety.

After an uneventful evening with nothing more than the common text message harassment, Marco and Jennifer awoke and decided to have some stress free fun for the day. "We went to the mall, and then to a movie. Then the text messages and calls started again," he said.

Jennifer answered Emanuel's calls in an attempt to appease the stalker by trying to keep him calm, a common tactic in stalking cases. Experts will tell you that it never works, and this case was no exception. Marco and Jennifer agreed to shut the phone off and "not deal with this guy today."

They arrived back at Marco's condominium and, after an enjoyable dinner, the two fell asleep at approximately 12:30 am. Marco had left his Springfield on the nightstand, chambered and ready to bark in the event there was trouble. Jennifer's little .22

lay quietly next to the larger Springfield, smaller in stature yet ready to roar to life if needed.

"That's when I heard it. It sounded like some kind of explosion outside. I was asleep and only remember the explosion. I jumped up and grabbed my gun. I had no idea what it was," said Marco. "I remember grabbing my gun and walking out of the bedroom into the living room," he said. Looking out the large window in front, Marco could see the silhouette of a large man "with the light behind him standing just outside on the balcony. It looked like a movie," he told me.

Not believing what was happening, and with absolutely no time to think, Marco decided to fire a warning shot into the wall between the window and the door in a futile attempt to scare away the intruder. POW! The XD roared to life, sending a 9mm Federal Hydra-Shok round into the wall just inches away from the prowler.

KABOOM, came the response, muzzle flash visible to Marco, as the loud crack of a Glock answered his warning, sending a round flying through the large window, shattering the glass and embedding itself just 6 inches from Marco's head into the wall behind him.

"…He just busted in the window like a rampaging madman. It was like a charging bull, man….He just kept coming," said Marco. "The curtains were flying and his arms were going like crazy." Shattering the glass and ripping through the curtains like a scene from a horror movie, with crazed eyes and gun in hand the intruder plowed over the loveseat directly in front of the window. BAM, BAM, BAM came the reply from Marco. "I just started firing my XD at him. He just kept coming man, he wouldn't stop. I was firing my gun, just firing without stopping and retreating down the hallway for cover. I knew I had to be hitting him. It was pitch black but there was no way I was missing him, but he just wouldn't stop." POW, POW, POW, POW, the Springfield was blazing away while the mad bull continued his relentless assault towards Marco.

Retreating to cover, and now alone in the bathroom, his adrenaline pumping, Marco could hear Jennifer screaming on the phone with 911. "I looked down at my gun and was searching for more ammo. I didn't know how many times I fired at him but I was scared to death he was going to bust in the room and I was going to have to keep fighting, and run out of ammo. I looked down at the gun and realized the slide wasn't locked back. I knew I only had like, one or maybe two rounds left, if that," he said.

The intruder fell, and Marco heard the sound. Cautiously exiting the bedroom, he would find Emanuel lying on the floor of his living room, bleeding. "Oh f---," whispered the intruder. What Marco saw next shocked him. Sitting on the floor, cradling the intruder's head in her lap was Jennifer, still on the phone with emergency operators, screaming and comforting her estranged husband.

That's when I knew it was her ex," Marco said. "Get your gun," he yelled to Jennifer as Emanuel lay wounded and bleeding on the living room floor. Fearing his ammunition was low enough to cost them their lives he realized she couldn't find her gun, but had lost it in the bed covers.

Marco put the muzzle of his XD less than one foot from the wounded man's head and yelled at him to give up his gun or he would kill him where he lay. With Emanuel lying with his hands crossed under his chest and face down on the living room

134

carpet, Marco could see him moving his arms in an attempt to reach for what Marco thought to be a gun. A desperate struggle began and within a few moments, Jennifer and Marco had taken the Glock from her estranged husband.

"I could see that he was reaching for another magazine, and when I took the gun I noticed it was damaged, and the magazine well was empty. As it turned out, his gun was damaged by one of my shots as he came through the window. His magazine was found by police on the loveseat in front of the window. He was looking for his other magazine to reload his gun," Marco said.

Within minutes, North Miami police were on scene. Marco attempted to open the front door, but couldn't. That's when he realized what the explosions were that awoke him. "He tried to shoot the deadbolt and doorknob in an attempt to open the door, but it didn't work. I guess he watches too much TV."

Emanuel was immediately flown to the local hospital where he received life-saving surgery to repair the wounds to his stomach and lower intestine. Marco had succeeded in hitting him six times in the neck and shoulder, two rounds to the stomach, groin and leg. It was Marco's shot to the leg, hitting Emanuel's femur bone, that dropped him to the carpet and ended the assault against Marco in his own home.

Marco was informed immediately by responding police and detectives that there were would be no charges against him. He told me that officers actually patted him on the back.

Emanuel was charged with five felonies including two attempted murder charges, armed burglary of an occupied dwelling, shooting or throwing a deadly missile in an occupied dwelling, and use of a firearm while committing a felony.

Since the event that almost ended his life, Marco has moved from the 9mm to a .40 caliber. He never carries less than two magazines of ammunition. He has since decided to move on with his life and has left Florida to begin his life anew in another state. He continues to work as a lifesaving paramedic. He and Jennifer are no longer together.

Chapter 12 - When the Shooting Stops

Kathy Jackson

Although the fantasy is that when you act in self-defense, the situation immediately resolves itself, reality is a bit different. Not every situation where a gun is pulled will result in shots being fired. Even if shots are fired, the criminal might not be hit; if he is hit, he might remain conscious and alert although physically unable (or emotionally unwilling) to fight back. There are a lot of possible outcomes that do not involve the good guy standing over a dead body. Regardless of the physical outcome, it's important to have a plan to maintain control of the situation until the authorities arrive.

Command Voice

Perhaps the most important scene-management tool is a good *command voice*.

A good command voice starts from deep in the belly, not from the throat. When humans are under stress, it is common for our vocal chords to tighten up, forcing our voices to sound high and squeaky. By its very nature, a high, squeaky voice sounds less serious, less authoritative, less worth heeding than a deep and powerful voice. To naturally lower your voice and also increase its volume, bring the sound up from your diaphragm in a solid, explosive sound. Consciously force your voice to be both loud and deep, coming from the belly and lower chest.

This loud, deep command voice does not come naturally to many of us, but it is worth practicing. One common hurdle to using our voices in this way is simple embarrassment, as in our culture we are taught from childhood to keep our voices low and unobtrusive in public. To counter this embarrassment, try practicing your command voice at a time and place when you cannot possibly be overheard or surprised by another person entering the room – such as when alone in your vehicle during your morning commute.

So now you know what your voice should sound like. But what should you say? I suggest you practice certain 'set phrases,' words that will come easily to you in a moment of stress and which can be easily understood by both assailant and potential witnesses. Some phrases you might practice:

"DON'T MOVE!"

"GET BACK!"

"DON'T TOUCH ME!"

"DROP THAT WEAPON!"

"SLOWLY ... RAISE YOUR HANDS!"

"STAY BACK! HE STILL HAS A WEAPON!"

"YOU! CALL THE POLICE! CALL AN AMBULANCE!"
(to a witness or bystander)

Obviously, each of these phrases has its place, and you will not use any phrase unless the situation warrants its use. The point is that by practicing them in advance, and mulling over when you might use them, they become part of your easily-accessed response routine. You won't stumble or bumble looking for what to say, or inarticulately gabble in your haste to say *something.*[1]   The words will come easily to your lips and will therefore sound more certain.

Each word should come out separately, individually, in an explosion of power that comes from the belly. Consciously pause between each word as you practice, knowing that under stress the tendency will be for these words to blend together and blur. Practice saying them loudly, clearly, and authoritatively.

Position of Advantage

Your body language should match your authoritative speech, creating a *command presence* that tells the assailant and the witnesses that you have taken control of the situation.

"Assume your assailant is still dangerous ... expect a conscious intruder to resist verbally and physically," warns Gila Hayes in her excellent book *Personal Defense for Women*.[2]

The late Jim Cirillo, famed survivor of more than a dozen shootouts during his time on the New York City Stakeout Unit during the late 1960s and early 1970s, enjoyed telling the story of a shooting involving another team on the squad who were armed with .38 Special revolvers, which were then standard issue in many departments. One of the involved officers fired five shots, while the other fired six shots, and all eleven shots hit the suspect in the neck or face at close range. After the shooting stopped, one of the officers called in to report the shooting. Cirillo wrote, "He stood over the downed and evidently dead robber and called in his description. 'I got a male black, 6'2" or 6'3", weight 270 to 300 pounds, age, uh, uh, uh 32 years.' With that the robber suddenly opened his eyes and said, 'Shit man, I'm only 26. Hey officer, can I have a tissue? I got blood in

1-For more about speech difficulties during high-stress encounters, see *On Combat* p 91-93
2-Gila Hayes, *Personal Defense for Women*, read in manuscript form in early 2009.

my nose.'" When given a tissue, the suspect blew his nose and a spent bullet plopped out onto the floor. The man then walked over to the ambulance under his own power and without assistance.[3]

As amusing as Cirillo's tale may be, it points up an important truth: even an apparently-dead attacker can suddenly "come back to life," and those that do can pose a risk to others. Never assume that the downed attacker is out for good.

If the attacker is down but still conscious, the danger is even more pronounced. Dr. Bill Lewinski, of the Force Science Institute, has performed several studies with downed suspects and the danger they pose to responding officers. In one early study, the person playing the suspect role was positioned face-down on the floor, with his hands underneath him, ready to roll or turn and present a firearm if the opportunity allowed. The average time it took him to make these threatening moves was about one-third of a second, which Lewinski stressed would likely be "faster than an average cover officer could react and shoot to stop the threat, even if the officer had his gun pointed, his finger on the trigger, and had already made the decision to shoot. In other words, the officer would stand little chance of being able to shoot first."[4]

With this in mind, if at all possible, even if the attacker is down, do not approach him. If you must give commands, give your commands from a defensible position. If cover or concealment is available, get behind it. As soon as possible, command the assailant into a position where he cannot easily see you or

3-Jim Cirillo, *Guns, Bullets, and Gunfights: Lessons and Tales from a Modern-Day Gunfighter*. Paladin Press, 1996. p 103-105.
4-Reported in Force Science News #113, accessed online at www.forcescience. org/fsinews/2009/01/force-science-news-113-new-study-explores-threats-posed-by-prone-suspects

tell what you are doing as your attention must necessarily be divided between controlling him and getting help on its way.

Call the Police

Ideally, you will call emergency services yourself to report the situation. Whether the assailant has remained on the scene or has fled, whether you fired shots or not, it is important that you – the armed citizen – are the first one to contact the authorities.

In *The Gun Digest Book of Concealed Carry*, Massad Ayoob tells the story of a self-defense case that went to trial eleven agonizing months after the initial encounter. Although the case resulted in an acquittal, it was a long ordeal for the citizen and his family. After relating the facts of the encounter and briefly explaining the progress of the trial, Ayoob writes, "This whole thing went the way it did after the gun was put away because the defendant didn't get his story in to the authorities before his antagonists did. The entire criminal justice system is geared on the assumption that whoever calls in first is the complainant, the *victim*. The good guy now, by default, becomes the bad guy: the *suspect*. The *perpetrator*. In situations like these, you're a contestant in what I've come to call 'the race to the telephone.' The winner gets to be the good guy, and the loser automatically becomes the bad guy." To avoid being caught in a similar situation, do your best to win the race to the telephone after an encounter.[5]

When you call 911, start by giving your location. Especially important if you dial via a cell phone, the address is the single most critical piece of information you can supply. As a police dispatcher of my acquaintance is fond of saying, "If you need help, I can send you the whole world – but I have to know where

5-Massad Ayoob, *The Gun Digest Book of Concealed Carry*, p 37-44.

to send it!" If you know the address, give the address. If you don't know the address, give the street name and the names of the nearest cross streets. If you don't know even that much, describe a local and prominent landmark and your relation to that landmark. And, as a lifetime habit, get in the practice of maintaining a continuous awareness of *where you are*, mentally checking off the address as you enter a building, and noting cross streets as you go about your business on the road.

When calling to report an intruder who has entered your home, *do not report the situation as a "robbery."* Instead, report "an intruder" or "an attack." The reason for this is that many people call 911 to report simple burglaries, so the dispatcher may reasonably believe that your call is a low-priority report of a non-threatening loss of property, not a plea for help involving an immediate threat to human life. Use words that make the true situation immediately clear.

Some of the most dangerous moments following a defensive shooting happen when the police arrive on scene. For this reason, take care to clearly describe yourself to the dispatcher, and reiterate that you are describing *yourself* as the victim. Be sure he or she understands that this description applies to the victim and not the assailant. Unless there is some powerfully overwhelming reason to do so, don't give a description of the assailant to the dispatcher because your first priority is to avoid getting shot as a criminal by responding officers. You can give the assailant's description to responding officers when they arrive. Such descriptions go astray often enough that it's worthwhile to avoid creating any cause for confusion.

The dispatcher is trained to keep the caller on the line until the police arrive on scene. However, once you have provided the important details – address, need the police, need an ambulance, number of people down, a description of yourself as the armed good guy – it is okay to set the phone down (don't hang up!) so you can concentrate on the other jobs you need to do. By leaving the phone off the hook, you maintain an open audio record of events even though you must concentrate on other important matters. Don't expect the dispatcher to be happy about this, but your first priority is to stay safe and you may not be able to do so if half your attention is on the phone.

If you must send a bystander or witness to contact the police, be very clear about *which* bystander you are sending. Point directly at the person and use command voice: "YOU! CALL THE POLICE. CALL AN AMBULANCE." Single the person out, look them in the eye, and make it plain that you expect them, personally, to do this task.

If a group of people surrounds you, pick someone else out of the crowd. Get that person's attention and say: "YOU! GO WITH HIM (or her). CALL THE POLICE. CALL AN AMBULANCE." By personalizing the task, you increase the chances that it will be performed. By sending a second person, you improve accountability for the first. If instead you simply call out, "Someone call the police," there's a very strong chance that each person in the crowd will think "someone" actually means "someone else." So assign the task to a specific person, and send along an accountability buddy if you can.

Waiting for the Police

As you await the arrival of police, stay in command of yourself and your emotions. Even if your assailant has departed, it is not yet time to relax. He may return. He may have associates who will crash onto the scene for revenge or rescue. Above all, you must remain alert for the arrival of the police officers who may have an incomplete description of the scene and who will naturally assume that the person with the gun (that's *you*!) is the primary threat they will need to control when they arrive.

Be aware that there may be a long delay before help arrives. The longer this delay lasts, the greater the fatigue you may experience as the rebound effect from the adrenalin dump kicks in. At the same time, the danger from the assailant increases with each passing moment, as he has time to think about his predicament and the likely consequences of his capture. Even if the assailant appears to be down and out, you must not relax your vigilance until the professionals have arrived to take control.

If possible, move behind cover or concealment in relation to the downed assailant, keeping him at gunpoint as you do so. Place an object such as a chair or a desk between you, or work around an open doorway rather than standing in the open. If you can place yourself so the assailant cannot easily see what you are doing, you will be somewhat safer than if you are positioned where every nuance of your expression and stance remains easily seen and immediately noticed.

While you are waiting for the police, and if you can do so safely, check yourself and have your loved ones check themselves and each other for injuries you might not have noticed in the heat of the encounter. Many law enforcement officers and soldiers tell stories of serious injuries that the victim did not realize had happened until after a deliberate, visual check.[6] If anyone is bleeding, stop the bleeding with direct pressure or a properly applied tourniquet and have the victim lie down with

---

6-David Klinger, *Into the Kill Zone*.

the injured part elevated above the heart if possible. Consider first aid training for the entire family as part of your reasonable preparation to survive dangerous situations. While it might save your life during or immediately after a lethal force encounter, a basic knowledge of first aid often comes in handy in more everyday circumstances too.

When the Police Arrive

The first rule for dealing with the police after a shooting is simply this: Don't get shot. To avoid getting shot, get the gun out of your hands at the earliest possible opportunity.

When the police arrive on scene, they will be amped up and full of adrenalin, ready to charge in with a full awareness of danger. For this reason, place yourself where the odds are best that *you* will see them before *they* see you. This will prevent you from suddenly swinging around with gun in hand when the police arrival startles you. Understandably, people who quickly turn toward the cops with gun in hand often get shot.

If you can do so safely, get the gun out of your hands before the officers arrive, or as soon as you see the first responding officer. You can reholster the firearm, keeping your hand on it in case the assailant tries to jump up at this point. Or if the assailant appears to be down and out, you can place the firearm on a shelf or table in front of you, within reach just in case the situation changes. Get your empty hands where the officers can see them, so they do not mistake you for a deadly threat.

If you are not able to get the gun out of your hands before the police enter the area, immediately drop the gun when told to do so. Do not argue. Do not try to protect the gun's finish. Simply drop the firearm as commanded, get your open palms where the cops can see them, and follow the officers' instructions to the letter.

Be a Good Witness

The police will enter the scene believing that they are investigating only one event, which is the shooting. At the earliest possible moment, it is vital to let the police know that there was a precipitating event, the criminal assault which caused you to reasonably fear for your life. You are the best witness to that criminal assault, and information about the assault will be critically important to your own legal defense.

At the same time, "A survivor who makes a lengthy statement to the first responder will probably relate incorrect information, especially about exact lengths of time, specific distances and other details," writes Gila Hayes in *Personal Defense for Women*.[7] An earlier chapter of this book detailed exactly why this is so, and a few minutes spent interviewing any defense attorney will simply cement your resolve not to talk yourself into jail following a shooting. The critical element here is to communicate enough information that the cops are prepared to gather evidence of the crime that was committed against you, but not so much that you begin confabulating details as your adrenalized brain is likely to do. Your legal position will be strongest when the evidence the police gather accurately and truly reflects the entire sequence of events that led to the shooting.

For this reason, lethal force expert Massad Ayoob urges people to describe the "active dynamic" of the situation to responding officers. The "active dynamic" is what happened that caused an upright and innocent person to reasonably believe lethal force was warranted. The active dynamic is *not* "I shot

7-*Personal Defense for Women*, reviewed in manuscript form.

him." The active dynamic *is* "he attacked me." Without adding any unnecessary details, take just one or two sentences to tell the officer what the criminal was doing, what crime was he in the very act of committing, that caused you to believe innocent life was in danger.

Ayoob also suggests framing your remarks thusly: "That person attacked me. If he survives, I'll sign the complaint. The witnesses are there (point them out) and the evidence is there (point it out). Officer, you know how serious this is; you'll have my full cooperation after I've spoken with counsel."[8]

For ease of memory, this can be consolidated into a five-word list: suspect(s), victim(s), evidence, witness(es), lawyer.

- ***Suspect(s)***. That person (or group of people) attacked me. If the attacker has fled the scene, give a description and point out the direction and means of travel.

- ***Victim(s)***. If the person (or group of people) who attacked me survive, I will sign the complaint; OR I will cooperate in identifying and prosecuting the assailant when he is caught. Don't proclaim yourself to be a victim – determining which person on scene is the true victim is the prerogative of the responding officers – but do make it clear that you are willing to help the prosecutor get a conviction for the crime which was committed against you. If any other people were injured and have not yet received medical attention, point them out; they, too, are victims.

- ***Evidence***. Point out any evidence that might not be immediately obvious, or that might walk away or otherwise evaporate. If you saw your assailant drop something in the bushes, say so. If something got kicked underneath a couch, or rolled underneath a vehicle, or fell to the middle of the

8-Notes taken during LFI-1 class taught by Massad Ayoob.

street where the crowd is beginning to gather, point it out. Don't assume that the cops will truly fine-tooth-comb the whole area, or that they'll look for evidence of one type of crime (the criminal's assault against you) while they are investigating another, more serious crime (a possible murder). Similarly, if you have bruises or marks on your body from the struggle, or if your clothing was torn during the assault, point it out and ask them to photograph it. If they don't know an assault was committed against you, they won't look for evidence of that assault, and therefore probably will not catalog apparently-unrelated objects or photographically preserve visual evidence that might help your situation.

• *Witnesses.* Point out any people who saw or may have seen what happened. Point out any people who heard or may have heard what happened. "Don't get involved" has become such a powerful cultural mantra that it's pretty much a given that most witnesses will slip away unless someone in authority spots them and encourages them to stick around.

• *Lawyer.* "Officer, you know how serious this is, and I am invoking my right to remain silent at this time. You'll have my full cooperation after I've spoken with legal counsel." Repeat the final sentence as many times as needed. Say nothing else.

Once you have communicated the active dynamic and the important basic factors to police – suspects, victims, evidence, and witnesses – it is time to close your mouth and leave the talking to your attorney. Depending upon the situation and perhaps the jurisdiction, the police may decide to arrest you on the scene, or they may allow you to go home to your family that night. In either case, your best opportunity to stay free, or to go free as soon as possible, is to calmly cooperate without saying anything else at this point. Do not speculate even if invited to do so. Do not get sucked into a lengthy conversation with anyone, police or not. Do not tell the full story. Stick with pointing out the critical information, then shut up and wait for your attorney.

"One Phone Call"

If you are arrested, you will receive the opportunity to make a phone call, sometimes even a series of phone calls, to let others know what has happened and where you are. Prepare your loved ones in advance to receive such a call, discussing practical questions such as whom you would expect them to contact on your behalf. Explain that if you need to make this phone call, you probably will *not* be able to give details of the situation over the phone, or tell the whole story right away, but that you will need them to organize your response team during the time when you cannot organize it yourself. While this conversation might be an awkward one to begin now, it would be far more awkward to have the conversation while you are in handcuffs and speaking to one another over the monitored and recorded phone in the sheriff's office. If your spouse or significant other is not comfortable in the "one call" role, or would be unsuitable for other reasons, find a trusted friend to do the task.

Make sure your one phone call will not be wasted on someone who will have no idea what to do next. When you ask someone whether they are willing to provide this service for you, give the person an emergency contact list of people who will need to be told about the situation. Make sure your friend has the name and phone number of an attorney they can contact on your behalf. If you have had professional firearms training, provide the name and phone number of your instructor, who may in turn be able to help mobilize a network of concerned and sympathetic firearms owners to provide the practical and emotional support you may need – especially if your local community is hostile to firearms ownership or self-defense. Prepare your friend for the call and help them understand how critical it is to get your legal and practical response team activated as soon as humanly possible.

Keep another copy of your contact list inside your gun safe where it is secure and easily accessible in the event of an emergency. That way, if your "one call" friend is not available, anyone with the combination to your safe will be able to obtain your contact list and get your response team activated.

One number on my personal response team belongs to the Armed Citizens' Legal Defense Network (ACLDN). Founded in 2008, the Network includes such luminaries as Marty Hayes, Massad Ayoob, Tom Givens, and Dennis Tueller. This organization exists to support the armed citizen during the hours and days immediately after a shooting, and to provide expert assistance to qualified defense attorneys both before and during trial. A phone call to ACLDN immediately after the event may help avoid mistakes or omissions during the immediate aftermath that can lead to significant (and costly) legal woes later.

Here is a suggested outline for a conversation with your primary "one call" contact:

1. I was involved in a shooting; I am OKAY and I love you.[9]

9-Obviously, you only need to add "I love you" if your one phone call is with a family member or significant other. If it is your significant other, "I love you" is one of the most important and life-affirming things you can say after a deadly force event.

2. I am in custody of _____ (police department where you are being held).

3. I have not called anyone else; can you handle contacting people for me?

4. Please find an attorney. The attorney can contact _____ (officer's name) through _____ (name of police department or other law enforcement agency) to discuss my case and get ahold of me.

5. I don't have time to tell you the whole story right now, and I'm still a little shaken up. But I am OKAY and I love you. (Do not give details about the event, even if asked.)

If you are not able to get ahold of your primary "one call" person who has your emergency contact list, and must instead call someone who has not been prepared beforehand to handle the immediate practical tasks, subtract "I love you" from the list above and add one more entry: "Can you please get ahold of (primary contact person) and let them know where I am? They'll know who else needs to be called."

Arrested?

Some folks may be frightened of the legal system following a self-defense shooting. This is entirely appropriate, but must not be blown out of proportion. Although an otherwise upstanding citizen may occasionally be convicted for using deadly force in self-defense, it is extremely unlikely outcome. Minor tangles with the legal system after a shooting are fairly common, but devastating outcomes are truly rare.

To reduce the already-low risk of a bad legal outcome following a shooting, a little intelligent preparation can go a long

And your loved ones need to hear it along with the reassurance that you really are okay.

way. Those who have attended a professional firearms training school (not just a state-mandated CCW class) find that the training will be tremendously helpful in reducing their chances of hitting an innocent bystander or making an unrealistic decision in the heat of the moment – and the personal contacts they make through the school will often stand them in good stead following a defensive gun use. If it is at all possible to work true professional training into your budget, I'd urge you to do so, considering the cost as a simple insurance equation.

Joining the Armed Citizens' Legal Defense Network is another intelligent move you can take beforehand. While the ACLDN is not insurance, it does offer its members immediate help with legal costs and practical issues immediately after a criminal encounter. The instructional resources available to members, especially the CDs sent to every member upon joining, are alone worth the cost of the membership. If the advice given in the CDs is followed, members have little chance of difficulty with the legal system even in gun-unfriendly areas. Further, the advantage of having access to free and truly expert advice following a shooting, and to free and truly expert testimony if the case goes to trial, simply cannot be overstated. Simply put, if your defensive gun use does go to trial, having experienced and qualified expert witnesses will be an essential cornerstone of your lawyer's strategy, and the experts provided by the ACLDN are some of the best (and best-known) in the industry.

Given the choice between surviving to fight for my freedom in an American court of law, or dying at the hands of a violent and sadistic criminal – I'll take court, every time. Wouldn't you?

Chapter 13 - Because I Needed the Money

Mark Walters

When Maria Harris, who was then the Managing Editor of Concealed Carry Magazine, asked me to contact a subscriber who she claimed had a story to tell, I had absolutely no idea what impact it would later have on me as a writer, a father and a human being.

Maria had asked me to contact a fellow USCCA member to discuss an incident he wanted to pass on to the magazine. I made contact with Mr. Erick Williams the following day by email and later that week by phone. Erick proceeded to tell me one of the most devastating accounts of criminal viciousness that I had ever heard. In fact the account was so devastating I had almost feared pursuing it for lack of ability to frame the words effectively enough to do justice to the victims. I was certainly faced with my most challenging column.

Erick had told me that Mr. Jorrick Landry wanted his story out there for the benefit of others and I agreed to a conference call that afternoon. The following account was told to me by Mr. Landry and was followed up by me with readings of the Jacksonville Florida Times Union newspaper accounts and police reports. It is one of the most harrowing experiences I have ever heard and I pray to God that no one ever find themselves in the absolutely terrorizing predicament the Landry family faced that horrible May night in Jacksonville, Florida.

MAY, 2006: Jacksonville, Florida

Jorrick Landry and his family can tell you first hand how difficult the life of a US Navy sailor can be. It entails long hours working when the ship is in port and long, strenuous weeks away from home while on sea duty – weeks that turn to months in the blink of an eye. As someone who has many friends and relatives who have spent time in the Navy, Jorrick's plight is one I have heard before. Wives keep busy through support groups, knowing that the tedious days alone running the household and taking care of the family in the father's absence can put a tremendous stress on even the strongest of relationships.

Jorrick had told me during the beginning of our discussion that the crime rate in his area was becoming of greater concern for him. Through much discussion with his wife, they agreed that the family would keep a firearm for self-defense during his lengthy absences at sea. As the day of his departure on yet another deployment rapidly neared, Jorrick and his wife Vernalise decided to attend a CCW class together so he could feel comfortable knowing his wife had a means of defending the family while he was away. After seeing one of Erick Williams' CCW instruction course advertisements, Jorrick and Vernalise signed up for class.[1]

Jorrick and his wife attended the CCW class on Saturday afternoon April 30, 2006, during which time they were taught the Florida statutes and basic firearm safety. Erick took them to the range and both passed the class together. Jorrick was not aware

---

1-Jacksonville Concealed Carry. (904) 759-1564. www.jacksonvilleconcealed-carry.com

that it was legal in Florida to keep a loaded gun concealed in a vehicle without a Florida CCW until Erick mentioned it during their instruction. After passing the class together and sending in their CCW paperwork, Jorrick and Vernalise now kept their revolver in the console of the family SUV for their protection, while waiting for their Florida licenses to arrive.

With the firearm instruction now out of the way, and feeling somewhat safer, Jorrick and Vernalise now turned their attention to the family activities during his upcoming deployment. They had seen an advertisement for a "day camp" for children at McGirts Park in Jacksonville and had decided to sign up the children. This activity would certainly give Vernalise some much-needed downtime while taking care of the family in Jorrick's absence. Vernalise had called the recreation center and was told that the applications were on a first-come, first-served basis. The woman on the other end of the phone had told them it was not unusual for parents to begin lining up in their vehicles just after midnight the night before to assure themselves one of the limited spots.

Early Saturday Morning, May 6

At approximately midnight on May 6, 2006, Vernalise set out for the park while Jorrick remained home with the 3 children. Shortly after her arrival and realizing that theirs was the only vehicle at the park, Vernalise called Jorrick to inform him that she was not comfortable waiting alone. Not wanting to miss the camp sign-ups, and concerned for his wife's well being and safety, Jorrick asked her to come home to pick up him and the children and they would make a fun night of it together as a family. The children were awakened and loaded into the SUV and the family set out for the park to assure themselves spots for the kid's camp.

The family arrived back at the park together around 1:30 am. Vernalise sat in the driver's seat with Jorrick in the passenger seat beside her. Zaccheaus, 7, settled in the middle of the back seat while 2-year-old Anaiyah hopped into her mother's lap in the front seat. Sitting alone in the far back of the SUV was 10-year-old Drevon, who was keeping himself busy with a video game.

The Face of Evil

Jorrick and Vernalise were discussing the fact that they were still the only folks waiting for camp sign up when he appeared. While she was talking to her husband, Vernalise suddenly yelled to Jorrick in shock at what she saw outside the passenger window just inches from and behind her husband. A young man in a mask and dark clothing had approached the passenger side window and pumped his shotgun, sending a live round into the chamber before screaming at Jorrick inside the vehicle to give him "everything he had."

With a loaded shotgun now pointed directly at his face, Jorrick offered the man his wallet. Desperately fearing for the lives of her children, Vernalise offered the crazed punk everything they had, including their SUV, but the robber growled, "Shut up, bitch!" Vernalise begged the man to leave them alone, telling him they had children in the car. Relating the story later, Jorrick said that at Vernalise's words about the children, the criminal's eyes "lit up like he hit the lottery."

The man immediately screamed back into the SUV through the slightly opened passenger window, "Kids? Let me see some mother-f---ing kids!" Jabray Davias Jones, 18 years old, then began forcing his way into the Landry family's SUV through the rear passenger side door, pushing 7-year-old Zacheaus across the back seat.

Time to Act

With a shotgun-wielding maniac inside his vehicle, Jorrick had to react to save the lives of his family. Thank God, he later told me, that Erick Williams had set him straight on the Florida law which allowed him to have a loaded gun in his vehicle for protection without a carry permit.

Looking behind and over his right shoulder in utter disbelief at the frightening events unfolding behind him, Jorrick Landry reached for the console and the handgun inside it, trying not to let the maniac threatening his family see what he was doing. Watching her husband fumble for the weapon and realizing she was in a fight for the lives of her children, Vernalise discreetly assisted Jorrick. Opening the console and breaking the thumb latch, Vernalise quickly and quietly handed the gun to Jorrick while dropping 2-year-old Anaiyah on the floor at her feet between the seat and the pedals.

Jorrick, now armed with a handgun, swung around to his right, placing the gun between his seat and the door, and began firing at Jabray Davias Jones as Jones entered the family's vehicle. Vernalise, having dropped Anaiyah to the floorboard at her feet and in a desperate and incredibly heroic attempt to save her family, reached for and grabbed the shotgun muzzle behind her and to the right, forcing it towards the floorboard in the back seat.

KABOOM! Jones squeezed the trigger on the shotgun, the explosion ripping into the floorboards of the SUV. KABOOM! A second shot roared out, both blasts going unnoticed by Jorrick, who continued firing, emptying his handgun into the now seriously wounded criminal who had invaded and threatened the lives of his family.

Out of ammunition, and during what seemed like an eternity, Jorrick watched as a wounded Jabray Jones tumbled back out of the SUV through the same door he had forced his way into just seconds earlier, striking the pavement with a thud. Jorrick had succeeded in hitting Jones multiple times in the groin area, leg, stomach and eye, with the shot to the eye lodging in his head directly behind the ear. The shot to the leg had penetrated through and traveled up Jones' arm, destroying his bicep muscle.

During the incredible violence and with unparalleled bravery, Vernalise had gained control of the shotgun, and she jumped out of the truck with baby Anaiyah. Zaccheaus jumped from the driver side rear passenger door and joined his mother and young sister, who were now safely outside of the vehicle. Drevon remained in the far rear of the SUV.

Taking Control

Jabray Davias Jones lay on the pavement gravely wounded and bleeding profusely. Vernalise, in control of the shotgun, threw it to Jorrick who was standing over the criminal as the young man bled out on the ground at his feet. Jorrick had dropped the empty revolver, racked another round into the chamber of the shotgun, and now held the wounded kidnapper on the ground with what seconds earlier had been the criminal's own weapon.

The wounded robber, with his own loaded gun pointed directly at him, began frantically fumbling inside his pants near his back for what Jorrick thought must surely be another weapon. "Stop reaching behind you!" Jorrick screamed at the man, "Stop it now!" Jorrick squeezed the trigger and opened up the shotgun with a deafening blast, tearing into the kidnapper's lower back near his waist, striking him near the kidney area at point blank range, and putting an immediate stop to the dying criminal.

Unbelievably, the young man was still alive when he uttered the words "Please, mister, no more." Jorrick told me that he knew that it was over when he saw Jones' body relax on the pavement. "I saw him give up," said Jorrick, still holding the shotgun over the now mortally wounded man on the ground.

"Why? Why did you do this to my family?" asked Jorrick.

"*Because I needed the money*," came the sickening reply from the dying Jabray Davias Jones.

Realizing he was in desperate need of medical attention and that his attempt to rob, kidnap and murder the Landry family had failed, Jabray Davias Jones asked Jorrick to reach into his pocket to retrieve his cell phone and "call for help." Holding the shotgun over Jones, Jorrick retrieved the wounded man's phone while continuing to hold him at gunpoint.

Not able to get service on Jones' phone, Jorrick yelled for Vernalise who was standing away from the vehicle with two of the children. She tossed her phone to Jorrick through the open car doors, and Jorrick was able to call for assistance while keeping the weapon trained on Jones.

Feeling confident and in total control of the situation, Jorrick Landry yelled for a roll call of his family one by one. Time seemed to stop when he realized that everyone had answered except for Drevon. Alone in the back seat and sitting directly behind the incredible violence that had unfolded seconds earlier inside the vehicle, Drevon was silent. Hearing emergency vehicles responding to the scene and still holding a shotgun at the wounded gunman, Jorrick looked inside the rear of the SUV to see his oldest boy slumped forward and bleeding against the rear of the seat in front of him.

The Crime Scene

During my interview with Jorrick, I was informed that a total of 10 to 12 minutes had elapsed since Jones began his terror against the family and the time he lay bleeding as police arrived.

Using a Maglite to alert the approaching vehicles to his location while he remained on the phone with emergency operators, Jorrick Landry did as instructed when the officers arrived. He lay on the ground, face down, while the officers gained immediate control of the crime scene.

The responding medical personnel, upon first arrival, rushed to the aid of the fallen criminal when Jorrick frantically alerted them to his wounded son in the rear of the vehicle. Drevon was rushed to Shands Jacksonville hospital in critical condition, wounded by a stray round that police would later determine came from a ricochet fired from his father's own gun during Jorrick's heroic efforts to save his family.

Homicide detectives removed Jorrick from the scene and took him to the police station where he was intensely interrogated about the events of the evening. Vernalise was questioned at the scene and sent to the hospital to be with her son.

Detectives, recognizing that Jorrick had moments earlier killed a violent criminal in the act of attacking his family and that he was distraught over his critically wounded son, allowed him to get regular updates from the hospital about Drevon's condition during the investigation. According to Jorrick, it was approximately 45 minutes later when he was informed that no charges would be filed against him and that detectives were considering his defensive use of force a justifiable homicide. He was quickly reunited with his family at Drevon's bedside.

Only hours after the incident and with his son in critical condition and in intensive care, Jorrick and Vernalise notified Erick Williams of what had occurred. Rushing to the hospital, Erick arrived to find Vernalise still wearing the blood-covered jeans she had worn during the attack. Jorrick approached Erick and collapsed into his arms, giving him a bear hug and thanking him repeatedly for informing him that they could legally keep the gun in the car. Jorrick broke down in tears in Erick's arms.

The Criminal's Intent

Although no one will ever truly know the final intentions of Jabray Davias Jones that night, clues left behind by the dead robber make it clear that he was not inclined to leave any witnesses. Jones was carrying what Jorrick described as "some sort of knapsack" with him during the commission of his crimes against the family. Police later told Jorrick the next day that the knapsack carried lighter fluid, tape, and dozens of shotgun shells. Basic detective legwork revealed that the shotgun was stolen, and although no hard proof existed, detectives told Jorrick that the pattern used was similar to other known crimes.

We can only speculate what might have happened if the criminal had been allowed to complete his planned attack.

EMS personnel on the scene described shotgun shells "falling out" of Jones' shirt as they cut it away at the crime scene. It was obvious that Jabray Davias Jones meant business.

The Robber

Jabray Davias Jones, 18 years old, expired on the scene as a result of Vernalise and Jorrick Landry's heroism and bravery in the face of pure evil. A student at Savannah State University, Jones had no known prior criminal record.

Police later told Jorrick that the violent nature of the crime, the weapon and the techniques Jones used during the attempted kidnapping and robbery suggest that Jones was no stranger to this type of behavior. It is probable, although not provable, that he had done this before and had never been caught. Similarities to other unsolved crimes were apparent to police.

One thing is certain; this criminal assailant will never again have the opportunity to harm anyone else. Predictably, those who knew him described him as a "good boy."

Drevon

Ten-year-old Drevon was severely wounded during the firefight that erupted in his family's SUV by what police later determined was a ricocheting round from his father's handgun. Jorrick later told Erick that during the violence in the vehicle, Jones had thrown up his arm in an attempt to block the incoming fire. Jorrick remembers Jones' hand striking his own hand or arm as he was firing. It was this action, he believes, that sent the stray shot into Drevon, striking him in the head at his left temple.

Though there were encouraging signs during the next week, Drevon passed away approximately one week after that horrifying night, never awakening.

The Family

Through these horrific events and through the loss of their beloved son, the Landry family has survived together through strength and faith. The events of May 6, 2006 have changed their lives forever.

As a retired law enforcement officer who has been through defensive shootings and their aftermath, Erick Williams has been a source of strength for Jorrick and his family, comforting them since that fateful night. Not long after the event, I asked Jorrick how he was coping with what had occurred and he told me that he is confident that his son knows that the outcome of the events of that night quite literally saved his entire family. Jorrick was given some time off by the United States Navy and is now back on active duty.

Follow-up

Since the appearance of this tragic story in Concealed Carry Magazine several years ago, I have received countless emails wishing the Landry family well and dozens of inquiries into how they are holding up. During subsequent conversations I can tell you that time will never heal the wounds this family has suffered.

Jorrick has told me that they have survived purely on their faith in God and their strength as a family. May God bless them

Chapter 14 - Sometimes Real Life Sucks!

Kathy Jackson

The hardest thing [to cope with has been] that with all that mental preparation I had done, all the mental rehearsals of what could happen and how would I react, I'd always been the victor and shot the bad guy and he's down and nobody else is hurt. I never prepared myself for people losing their lives. – *Andy Brown[1]*

When we visualize potential scenarios, it's always easy to picture everything as sweetness and light: everyone hails us as the hero, the scum is clearly scum, no good people get hurt, the masses cheer and the cops slap us on the back in glee that another criminal is off the street. But real life isn't always so facile. Your criminal scumbag might be someone else's 15-year-old child. Your best heroics might not be enough to save the life of someone you love. The cops might need to take you into custody to sort out the conflicting accounts of what happened, and they might even charge you with a criminal offense. You might not know even the physical outcome until days or weeks after the event, and it might literally be months or years until you know the legal outcome. Be aware of these negative possibilities, but don't let them paralyze you. Instead, let them motivate

---

1-Personal notes taken by the author during a presentation given by Andy Brown during LFI-1 class at the Firearms Academy of Seattle in June 2009.

you to build the kind of solid mindset you will need to survive after a deadly force encounter. Others have faced this type of thing and survived; you can, too.

Despite the horror of the events he faced that night, and although he and his family know the pain of losing Drevon will never go away, Jorrick Landry has been able to make his peace with the outcome. It wasn't an easy path. Indeed, even an otherwise ideal outcome to a high-stress lethal encounter can leave the survivors facing a bewildering mix of thoughts and emotions. The good news is that those who are forewarned about those reactions tend to do a bit better in the long run than those who are blindsided by their own unexpected thoughts and feelings.

Knowing in advance which reactions are common and *normal* helps prevent survivors from bottling emotions, living in denial and hiding secrets they are unable to speak even in the recesses of their own minds. The truths we are unable to speak often turn into a slow, systemic poison that damages family relationships and destroys mental health.

In his excellent book, *On Combat*, Lt. Col. Dave Grossman gives one surprising example of how this dynamic can work:

"The first response of most people upon seeing sudden, violent death is relief; they are relieved that it did not happen to them. Say your partner or your buddy is killed and your first thought is, 'Thank God it wasn't me.' Later, when you reflect on your first response, how do you think that will make you feel? Guilty. You are consumed with guilt because nobody ever told you that the normal response of most people upon seeing sudden violent death is to focus on themselves, and to feel relief.

It is similar to when the stewardess on an airliner tells [passengers] that if there is a loss of cabin pressure, oxygen masks will drop down, and they should put theirs on before they help small children. The first response of the organism is to take care of itself first, and that is okay, because that is simply the law of nature.

If you know in advance that it is normal upon seeing trauma and death, to think, 'Thank God it wasn't me,' then that thought will not have the power to hurt you later. That is the first debriefing principle: 'You are only as sick as your secrets.'" [2]

With that thought in mind – you are only as sick as your secrets – the purpose of this chapter is to give you a glimpse of the sorts of things that might affect you after a shooting. As with the physiological reactions to sudden danger outlined in an earlier chapter, not everyone will experience all of the reactions listed in this chapter. Some will experience only the physical reactions related to the adrenalin release, and those only for a few days and mildly. Others may experience the full range of possibilities in profound depth. In either case, beginning the journey with realistic expectations about self-defense and with a solid understanding of society's reaction to the use of lethal force can help survivors maintain an even keel through these potentially stormy waters.

In some ways, dealing with the aftermath of a deadly force event may be somewhat similar to moving through the stages of grief. Not everyone experiences a loss with the same depth of emotional feeling, but nearly everyone does move through a similar series of issues to a greater or lesser degree. Some

2-*On Combat*, p 264-265

people move through the issues very quickly, while others take more time to intensely process each stage. Both are equally normal and healthy.

It is important to note here that the vast majority of people who experience a traumatic event will be just fine afterward. Some people have an easy adjustment, some a more difficult one, but the vast majority makes their peace with the situation and moves on. Many are even stronger for having endured and prevailed.

Immediate emotional responses

Immediately after a deadly encounter, one common reaction is *euphoria*. The survivor feels "on top of the world," happy and pleased. It's important to note that most survivors will tell you that this feeling does not happen because you have *killed*, but because you have *survived*. You faced one of the most horrible events a human being can face, and you are still on this earth. You lived.

Firearms great Jeff Cooper famously said that after a shooting, your beer tastes colder, your bed feels warmer, and jokes are funnier. It was his experience that shooting an enemy was an overwhelming positive, something to be rewarded and celebrated. "There is nothing wrong with winning a fight," he wrote. "There is a great deal wrong with losing one."[3] In fact, Cooper enjoyed making fun of what he called the "modern fantasy" of post shooting trauma. He once wrote: "...the example of George Patton is illuminating. You will recall that he got into a fire fight down in Mexico when Pershing was looking for Pancho Villa.

3-*Cooper's Commentaries*, volume 4, issue 7, June 1996

When asked later how it felt to kill a man, Patton responded, 'I felt exactly the way I felt when I landed my first swordfish.'"[4]

As powerful as the feeling may be, this initial euphoria does not always last long, as the reality of the situation and the practical details that surround it begin to sink in.[5] Indeed, it's often followed by an equally strong backlash, where the survivor is sickened by their own first reaction. Grossman writes, "After a horrific experience, such as the loss of a partner or buddy, it can be a powerful shock to hear yourself think, 'Thank God it wasn't me.' Then the shock changes to shame, which makes you think, 'I wish it was me. I want it to be me....'"[6] This feeling can also affect those who had to shoot someone they knew, or those whose actions failed to save someone they loved.

Closely related to this, and perhaps an understandable side effect of adrenalin-jumbled memories, is another common reaction: self-blame. Survivors often wonder if there was anything more they could have done to prevent the situation or avoid it, if there were any actions they could have taken to improve the outcome, if there was anything at all they could have said to their loved ones at the beginning of the day that it's just too late to say now. Because no human being is perfect, everyone has something for which they might feel *regret*, and it's common in the face of an overwhelming negative situation to dwell on those things, and to then shoulder far more blame than is truly warranted. Because memories of the traumatic event are often jumbled, and because good people truly fear doing the wrong thing, some survivors immediately assume that the missing gaps

4-*Cooper's Commentaries*, volume 4, issue 1, January 1996
5-The initial euphoria does endure for some people, as Cooper's experience attested. That, too, is normal and not a sign that something is wrong. See *Into the Kill Zone*, p 217, to read another survivor's experience of satisfaction and even elation following a shooting.
6-*On Combat*, p 269

in their memories are covering up for their own mistakes: "It's all my fault. I didn't do *this* or *that* one thing that would have made the outcome perfect."

Again, not everyone feels either immediate euphoria or the backlash of shame and self-blame that often follow it. But some do. It is a normal feeling, and *it does not necessarily mean you did anything wrong.* Even in cases where a different action or set of actions from a survivor might have created a better outcome, it's important to remember that the true blame for the event and any part of its outcome does not belong to you or to any other innocent person; it belongs to the criminal, and only to the criminal.

This same basic emotional dynamic often also plays out in the minds of loved ones as well as survivors. Unfortunately, unless the loved ones were present during the event, the loved ones will usually be experiencing these reactions on a different time schedule than the survivors do. What this means is that *your* initial euphoria may have worn off, and you might be deeply into the "I wish it was me" phase just as your loved one learns you have survived. Their immediate reaction is relief, and they look you in the eye and say, "Thank God it wasn't you!" Though they say this with love and profound thankfulness, it can be hard for the survivor to hear *at that point,* because the survivor may have already moved beyond that feeling. These differing time schedules for dealing with the event can cause the beginnings of a chasm to open between you and your loved ones, just at the time you need each other most. For this reason, it's important to be aware of the dynamic at play here, so that if it does happen to you and to people you love, you are better able to move beyond it and come together for healing.

Another reaction that might come from a loved one is *anger*. If they first hear about the event in your absence, they may feel that initial relief at your survival, and then be deeply into a negative emotional backlash by the time you reach home. Again, this does not happen to everyone, but it does happen to some, and it's worthwhile to calmly consider it now, while your own emotions aren't jumbled. If your spouse or other loved one does react in this way, ask yourself, "Who are they really angry *at*?" Are they really angry at you? No. They are angry at the world that put someone they love in danger. They are angry that someone tried to harm a person they care about, and in the immediate aftermath they may displace that anger onto you.[7] Again, knowing this might happen can help prepare you to love and cherish each other despite the confusion of feelings.

Immediate physical responses

After a deadly encounter, survivors almost universally report some physical reactions to the stress of defending themselves from a life-threatening event. These physical reactions may take days or weeks to subside, and – again – they are normal and not a sign that something is wrong.

Sleep disturbances are foremost among these early physical reactions. Simply put, the body reacts to the naturally-produced adrenalin cocktail just as surely as it must to any other mix of powerful chemicals. The night of the shooting, and perhaps for many nights to follow, survivors often have trouble getting to sleep or trouble staying asleep. They may be haunted by nightmares or bad dreams, or they may simply have trouble "settling down" to slumber. If the encounter happened in the survivor's own home, or began while the survivor was sleeping, these

7-*On Combat*, p 269

physical reactions may be intensified by feelings of vulnerability. As one survivor reported,

"The first day, everything was so pumped up that I couldn't get to sleep. I'd been up well over twenty-four hours when I finally got back home. I wanted to go to sleep, but I was just so pumped up that I couldn't. I was zombied into the TV, just clicking channels, not even thinking about it. The next few days were like that, too. I'd try to go to sleep, but then I'd start to think about the shooting, and boy, there went my adrenaline right back up to that spot where it was right after it happened. Then, when I finally did fall asleep, I'd wake up after about four hours, think about the shooting, and get charged up again, which made it hard to go back to sleep." [8]

For those whose encounters took place toward the end of the day or during the evening hours, the sleep disturbances can be much more profound, in part because dealing with the immediate aftermath can take many hours and utterly prevent going to bed that night – immediately throwing your normal sleep rhythm severely off schedule.

This initial difficulty with sleeping *can* cascade into a later drug or alcohol problem, but it needn't do so. One early intervention that truly works for preventing such a cascade is simply to wear the body out with exercise in the days after the event. A vigorous workout can help process the physical aftereffects of the adrenalin dump and provide natural relief for stress-related problems with sleep during this early stage. By choosing the natural stress relief of vigorous physical activity immediately after the initiating event, you may be able to prevent a later,

---

8-*Into the Kill Zone*, p 226

highly annoying seesaw between sleep-deprived exhaustion and drugged slumber.

In addition to problems falling asleep or problems staying asleep, some survivors report difficulty with nightmares. Again, this is a normal response to a frightening or angry encounter, and not a sign that anything is "wrong." It is simply the brain's way of processing the excess energy – and as with other difficulties with sleep, it tends to lessen or entirely disappear in the face of vigorous physical activity during the day.

Reactions to society's reaction

Moving beyond the immediate reactions into more long-term responses, we find that the bulk of a survivor's emotional landscape following a lethal encounter are reactions, not to the event itself, but to societal perception of the event and the related social interactions that follow.

According to lethal force expert Massad Ayoob, every survivor of a gunfight that he has ever interviewed has universally experienced two reactions. First, all of them experienced sleep disturbances during the time immediately following their event. Second, every one of them experienced something Ayoob calls the "mark of Cain," the perception that others were aware of the event, and thinking of the survivor as "a killer," or as "that person who was involved in the news story last month."[9] Put simply, the mark of Cain has little to do with the survivor personally; it is simply a tag for the survivor's reasonable awareness that others are reacting to the survivor differently than they once did.

In June 1994, Andy Brown, who was then a 25-year-old senior airman assigned to bicycle patrol as a military policeman,

9-Notes taken during an LFI-1 class taught by Massad Ayoob.

was involved in a shooting at Fairchild AFB in Washington state. During that event, the attacker used a MAK-90 rifle to take the lives of five people and wound many others. Brown, armed with a Beretta 9mm handgun, peddled to the scene as soon as the call came in and found the attacker in the very act of firing the rifle at innocent people. As the attacker began shooting toward Brown, Brown dropped into a marksman's kneel to engage the attacker at a distance of approximately 70 yards. Four shots rang out, and two of the shots struck home: one hit the attacker's shoulder, and the other nailed him right between the eyes. The attacker fell lifeless, and Andy Brown became the hero of an otherwise very ugly day.

Fifteen years after the event, Andy Brown spoke to an audience of LFI-1 students at the Firearms Academy of Seattle. As he discussed the aftermath of the shooting, Brown noted, "It did become my identity for a number of years. That's one of the reasons why I got out of the Air Force. Every new base I went to, they knew who I was before I got there, and I couldn't escape it. You're always 'that guy from Fairchild.' Now I don't have a whole lot of friends outside of my family and they all know what happened. But [when meeting new people], I try not to bring up the story because it's good to have people learn who I am prior to knowing what I did."[10]

As with other survivors of lethal force encounters, Brown had to cope with negative news coverage and unpleasant comments from people who did not understand. "The media is not friendly to law enforcement or gun owners," he noted with wry understatement. "And then there was also the letters to the editor: why didn't I shoot the gun out of his hand?" As the audience reacted with

---

10-Presentation given during LFI-1 class at the Firearms Academy of Seattle in June 2009.

unbelieving laughter to this comment, Brown said dryly, "Yeah, that's what I thought too."

While military and law enforcement personnel tend to have supportive peers, ordinary citizens do not often enjoy the same advantage to the same extent. Even following an utterly justified shooting, church members may find themselves shunned by their previously-supportive network of religious friends; employees may find co-workers speaking nastily about them behind their backs (or they may find themselves out of a job); and on the home front, other parents may prevent their children from playing with the child of "a murderer." Put plainly, just at the time when you may perceive a great need for social affirmation, you may find yourself instead subject to a maelstrom of negative interactions including the loss of previously-treasured friendships.

This loss of social connections can be absolutely devastating to those who did not expect or anticipate it, and difficult enough for those who *did* realistically expect some unpleasant reactions from friends, neighbors, relatives, and co-workers. Is it any wonder that many survivors of deadly encounters report that they have experienced depression, feelings of social isolation, sexual dysfunctions, appetite disturbances, and even drug or alcohol abuse? Contrary to popular belief, these symptoms do not indicate that the survivor is experiencing a sense of guilt about the shooting. Rather, they are normal reactions to repeated, overwhelmingly negative social encounters. A survivor can feel quite comfortable with the decision to use lethal force, and may even feel outright satisfaction with the criminal's death, but still have difficulty coping with the change in social status that often follows such an event. After all, humans are social creatures, and we naturally react very strongly to strong social pressures. And the taboo against killing another human being is just about the strongest social pressure of all.

If you are serious about using a firearm to defend your life, and want to be prepared to cope with the social aftermath of doing so, it may help to consciously cultivate a secondary social network among those who are supportive of self-defense and firearms use. These understanding friends may easily become your psychological lifeline following a deadly encounter.

Building a bulletproof mind

Lt. Col. Dave Grossman teaches a popular seminar for law enforcement and military personnel, "Building a Bulletproof Mind." In that seminar, Grossman outlines several important steps people can take in advance of any traumatic situation to build what he calls a "bulletproof mind" – that is, a solid mental and emotional framework which can prepare the individual to survive a deadly encounter and to withstand the societal pressure which may follow. Perhaps the single most powerful unifying theme in these seminars is this: Denial is the enemy. Grossman stresses that denial has no survival value, and contends that being prepared to cope with deadly violence means refusing to engage in denial even when denial would be more immediately comfortable.

In *On Combat*, Grossman writes, "Denial kills you twice: once because you are physically unprepared at the moment of truth and might die in the incident; twice because you are psychologically unprepared and, even if you physically survive, you are likely to be a psychiatric casualty when your 'house of cards' collapses."[11]

11-Dave Grossman, *On Combat*, p 174

After noting that some people are profoundly distressed by killing, while others aren't, Grossman believes that the degree of prior preparation is a key factor. He claims that four things are held in common by people who cope well:

- They have been previously "stress inoculated" with realistic training;
- They have a strong internal locus of control, and believe that they have both the power and the ability to affect the outcome of the situation;
- They have a strong personal faith; and
- They are able to control their own emotions (which Grossman notes does not mean being unwilling or unable to talk about the precipitating event).

Grossman further says that one goal of inducing stress during training is to help participants avoid post-traumatic stress disorder (PTSD). He notes that according to the *Diagnostic and Statistical Manual of Mental Disorders*, one non-optional marker for PTSD is feeling "intense fear, helplessness, or horror" during the precipitating event. Grossman contends that if there is no extreme fear response during the event, there simply cannot be any PTSD afterward. He adds that even those who did experience an intense fear reaction will be able to cope afterwards if they consciously strive to de-link their emotional reactions from the memory of the event, not by avoiding all memories of the situation but instead by talking it out and coming to terms with what happened.

Similarly, the late Jim Cirillo, who survived over a dozen shooting events himself and observed the aftermath of many others during his time on the New York City Stakeout Unit, recommended that people who may go in harm's way must be mentally and emotionally prepared to do so. In his classic book *Guns, Bullets, and Gunfights*, he penned a list of specific factors which he believed would indicate a person was prepared to cope with high-stress lethal encounters. Cirillo's recommendations were tailored for those who would choose officers to become involved in SWAT teams and other units with a high likelihood of being involved in combat situations. He observed that the most successful gunfighters on the Stakeout Unit:

- Were competitive shooters with a high degree of skill
- Were successful hunters who got their quota every year
- Loved firearms and collected them
- Reloaded ammo
- Loved outdoor sports
- Were family men
- Were outgoing and liked people
- Had great compassion for the underdog, including helpless victims of crime.[12]

Massad Ayoob, who for decades has studied and reported upon ordinary citizens who lawfully use lethal force in self-defense, has also developed a sort of checklist based upon his many years of experience in interviewing survivors. In his LFI-1 classes, Ayoob notes the following observations about survivors of violent events:

- Law enforcement officers generally cope with the aftermath of violence better than others do. Ayoob attributes this to the fact that cops have a supportive peer group already in place, and their social surroundings are set up to deal with similar events.
- Women generally cope better than men. Ayoob notes

12-Jim Cirillo, *Guns, Bullets, and Gunfights: Lessons and Tales from a Modern-Day Gunfighter*, chapter 5. Paladin Press, 1996.

that there is little or no social expectation that a woman will tackle a man twice her size with her bare hands, or take a punch "like a man." As a result, women often experience a slightly more supportive social environment after a shooting than their male peers.

• Religious people generally cope better than the non-religious. There is a freedom and a power in being able to look in the mirror and say, "The Highest Judge of all has found me not wanting." Again, since so many of the worst effects happen as a response to society's reaction, having that social armor in place may help protect the survivor from the most painful aftereffects of using deadly force.

There does appear to be a single, unifying factor in each of the lists produced by these experienced and thoughtful men: those who unflinchingly consider the ramifications of using deadly force and who have a strong social network to support them in their resolve seem to cope best during the aftermath. This may give the thoughtful reader a place to start.

In discussing the psychological symptoms of post-shooting trauma – depression, appetite disturbances, substance abuse including pharmacological cascade, social withdrawal and isolation, sexual dysfunctions, sleep disturbances, and flashbacks – Ayoob notes one crucial point. "Victims suffer more than victors," he contends. Each of these symptoms is more common, and more severe, among *victims* of violent crime than they are among *survivors* of violent crime. He continues, "I would rather be the defendant than exhibit A. I would rather bear the mark of Cain than the mark of Abel."[13] So would I, brother. So would I.

13-Notes taken during an LFI-1 class taught by Massad Ayoob.

In the end, each person must come to terms with what they are willing to do to protect themselves and those they love. And in the end, every determined survivor must be able to say with a pure heart and a clear conscience: Human life is worth defending.

Bibliography

Artwohl, Alexis & Christensen, Loren

Deadly Force Encounters: What Cops Need To Know To Mentally And Physically Prepare For And Survive A Gunfight by Dr. Alexis Artwohl, PhD. and Loren W. Christensen. Paladin Press 1997. ISBN 0873649354

Ayoob, Massad

In the Gravest Extreme: The Role of the Firearm in Personal Protection by Massad F. Ayoob. Police Bookshelf 1980. ISBN 0936279001

Stressfire: Gunfighting for Police: Advanced Tactics and Techniques by Massad F. Ayoob. Police Bookshelf, 1986. ISBN 0936279036

The Gun Digest Book Of Concealed Carry by Massad Ayoob. Gun Digest Books 2008. ISBN 0896896110

Bates, Lyn

Safety for Stalking Victims: How to save your privacy, your sanity, and your life by Lyn Bates. iUniverse 2001. ISBN 0595181600

Cirillo, Jim

Guns, Bullets, And Gunfights: Lessons And Tales From A Modern-Day Gunfighter by Jim Cirillo. Paladin Press 1996. ISBN 0873648773

Hall, John & Patrick, Urey

In Defense of Self and Others...: Issues, Facts & Fallacies-The Realities Of Law Enforcement's Use Of Deadly Force. Carolina Academic Press 2005. ISBN 1594600546

Grossman, Dave & Christensen, Loren

On Combat: The Psychology and Physiology of Deadly Conflict in War and in Peace by Lt. Col. Dave Grossman with Loren W. Christensen. Warrior Science Publications 2008. ISBN 0964920522

Gutmacher, Jon

Florida Firearms – Law, Use, and Ownership. Warlord Publishing 2008. Order from publisher at 200 N. Thornton Ave.,

Orlando, FL 32801 or online from www.floridafirearmslaw.com
Hayes, Gila
Personal Defense for Women: Practical Advice for Self Protection by Gila Hayes. Gun Digest Books 2009. ISBN 1440203903
Jamison, Kevin
Missouri Weapons and Self Defense Law, Merril Press 2003. ISBN 0936783370. Order from 2614 NE 56th Terrace, Gladstone, MO 64119-2311or online from www.kljamisonlaw.com
Klinger, David
Into the Kill Zone: A Cop's-Eye View of Deadly Force, by David Klinger. San Francisco, CA. Jossey-Bass, 2004. ISBN 0787986038
Korwin, Alan
Gun Laws of America, Bloomfield Press 2005. ISBN 1889632147. Order from Bloomfield Press, 4848 E. Cactus, #505-440, Scottsdale, AZ 85254, or online from www.gunlaws.com
Miller, Rory
Meditations on Violence: A Comparison of Martial Arts Training & Real World Violence by Rory Miller. YMAA Publication Center, 2008. ISBN 1594391181
Proctor, Mike
How to Stop a Stalker, Mike Proctor. Prometheus Books 2003. ISBN 1591020913
Thompson, George & Jenkins, Jerry
Verbal Judo: The Gentle Art of Persuasion. Harper Paperbacks, 2004. ISBN 0060577657
Van Wyk, Charl
Shooting Back: the right and duty of self-defence. Christian Liberty Books 2001. ISBN 0620281200
Workman, Dave
Washington State Gun Rights and Responsibilities, D&D Enterprises. Order from D&D Enterprises, P.O. Box 1638, North Bend, WA 98045 or online from www.danddgunleather.com

Resources

Armed Citizens Legal Defense Network, LLC
PO Box 400
Onalaska, WA 98570
(360) 978-5200
www.armedcitizensnetwork.org

AWARE (Arming Women Against Rape and Endangerment)
PO Box 242
Bedford MA 01730-0242
(877) 672-9273
www.AWARE.org

Firearms Academy of Seattle
PO Box 400
Onalaska WA 98570
(360) 978-6100
www.firearmsacademy.com

Force Science Institute
124 East Walnut Street
Suite 120
Mankato, MN 56001
(507) 387-1290
www.forcescience.org

Lethal Force Institute/Police Bookshelf
PO Box 122
Concord NH 03302-0122
(800) 624-9049
www.ayoob.com

No Nonsense Self-Defense, LLC
Marc MacYoung
200 S. Wilcox St., #124
Castle Rock, CO 80104
www.nononsenseselfdefense.com

United States Concealed Carry Association
Delta Media LLC
N173W21298 Northwest Passage Way
Jackson WI 53037
(877) 677-1919
www.usconcealedcarry.com

Kathy Jackson is the managing editor of Concealed Carry Magazine. An instructor at the Firearms Academy of Seattle in Washington state, she takes special pleasure in helping other women learn to shoot. Visit her website at www.corneredcat. com.

Mark Walters is a nationally published magazine columnist penning "The Ordinary Guy" column for Concealed Carry
Magazine. In 2002, he survived a potential deadly street encounter because he was lawfully armed. Mark is a vocal second
amendment activist and brings freedom to the nation's airwaves
every week as the host of the nationally syndicated Armed
American Radio program. (www.armedamericanradio.org)